# LOUVRE

## VISITOR'S GUIDE

Françoise Bayle

art
lys :

Cover: LEONARDO DA VINCI, *Portrait of Lisa Gherardini del Giocondo*,
known as *La Gioconda* or *Mona Lisa* (detail), circa 1503-1506. Oil on wood, 77 x 53 cm
View of the Cour Napoléon
and the pyramid (architect: I.M. Pei) at night
Pages 4 and 5: Cour Marly
Page 6: THE LOUVRE OF PHILIPPE AUGUSTE, 12th century, foundations of the fortress and towers
Pages 8 and 9: museum plans

EDITORIAL CO-ORDINATION: DENIS KILIAN
GRAPHIC DESIGN AND LAYOUT: MARTINE MÈNE
PLANS: THIERRY LEBRETON, DOMINIQUE BISSIÈRE
PICTURE RESEARCH: CHRISTIAN RYO, EMMANUELLE GRAFFIN
PRODUCTION: PIERRE KEGELS

PHOTO CREDITS:
RMN: 12, 14, 27, 39, 47, 62, 74, 78, 79, 82, 88, 89, 91, 96, 99. RMN/Arnaudet D.: 33, 42, 44, 49,
51, 57, 67, 72, 73, 80, 88, 99, 100, 102. RMN/Arnaudet/Blot: 11. RMN/Arnaudet/Schormans: 64.
RMN/Beck-Coppola M.: 4, 100, 104. RMN/Bellot M.: 77, 91. RMN/Berizzi J. G.: 30, 44, 73, 76,
77, 90, 103. RMN/Bernard P.: 39. RMN/Blot G.: 19, 34, 35, 36, 43, 49, 50, 54, 61, 64, 68, 69, 80,
81, 82, 86. RMN/Blot/Jean: 42, 94. RMN/Bréjat H.: 33. RMN/Chuzeville: 12, 17, 18, 19, 20, 21,
22, 98, 101. RMN/Hatala B.: 83, 84. RMN/Jean C.: 13, 56, 59, 60, 70, 74, 86.
RMN/Jean/Lewandowski: 58. RMN/Jean/Schormans: 28. RMN/Larrieu Ch.: cover.
RMN/Lewandowski H.: cover, 10, 14, 15, 16, 18, 19, 20, 23, 24, 25, 26, 28, 40, 41, 45, 46, 48, 51,
52, 55, 59, 62, 63, 66, 68, 70, 72, 75, 89, 93. RMN/Lewandowski/Ojeda: 29. RMN/Mathéus: 102.
RMN/Ojeda R. G.: 16, 31, 32, 40, 42, 53, 56, 65, 71, 78, 80, 87, 92, 95, 97. RMN/Ojéda/Néri: 96.
RMN/Raux F.: 35, 38. RMN/Rose C.: 6. RMN/Schormans J.: 60, 66

ISBN: 2-85495-172-7
© ARTLYS 2001

# CONTENTS

# From a fortress to a museum: eight centuries of history

In its eight centuries of existence, its walls have witnessed numerous events in French history - from the assassination of Coligny, the death of Henri IV to the second marriage of Napoleon I, and every sovereign would attempt to leave his mark on the Louvre.

It was at the end of the 12<sup>th</sup> century that Philippe Auguste built a fortified castle on a site already named Louvre. Nearly two centuries later, this austere fortress was turned into a royal residence by Raymond du Temple, architect to Charles V, who transformed it into a "palace as spruce and as brilliant as an enamel". However, the Hundred Years' War and the châteaux on the banks of the Loire kept the subsequent kings away from the Louvre which thus became an arsenal and a prison. When François I decided to stay more often in his "pleasant town and city of Paris", he had major work carried out which would turn it into a real Renaissance palace - work that would be continued by his successor, Henri II.

Another equally royal project would long change the architectural future of the Louvre: the new Palais des Tuileries commissioned by Catherine de' Medici in 1564, six hundred metres from the Louvre, led to the idea of linking the two palaces; this became known as the "grand design". At the end of Henri IV's reign, the two buildings were linked, on the Seine side, by the famous Grande Galerie which borders the river. Work continued during the reign of Louis XIII and Louis XIV - Lemercier doubled the size of the Lescot wing and the colonnade designed by Claude Perrault was built; however, the Sun King focused all his attention on the work being carried out twenty kilometres from Paris, at Versailles. A period of neglect thus ensued, during which the Louvre was literally invaded by a wide range of occupants: artists, of course, housed there since Henri IV, together with a number of institutions, and also traders who set up their stalls almost everywhere.

At the end of the 18<sup>th</sup> century, the architectural history of the Louvre became inevitably linked with the concept of a museum. Throughout Europe, the idea of exhibiting the large collections belonging to the princes and popes to the general public was being increasingly envisaged. Within this sphere of influence, the Comte d'Angiviller, in charge of the King's Buildings, decided in 1776 to transform the Grande Galerie into a museum - the Academy of Painting, situated at the Louvre, had in fact been regularly exhibiting work by its members in the Grande Galerie for many years. The museum was prevented from opening due to the Revolution, but the Constituent Assembly adopted d'Angiviller's ideas and officially created the *Muséum Central des Arts* on 6 May 1791, which was inaugurated on 10 August 1793.

With the victories of Napoleon I, masterpieces flooded in from the whole of Europe to hang on its walls, that is, until 1815 when the allied powers demanded the restitution of their goods. In 1866, Napoleon III was credited with accomplishing the "grand design" by linking the Palais des Tuileries to the Louvre through the construction of the north wing based on Visconti's, and later Lefuel's plans. However, in 1871, the Commune set fire to the Tuileries: the Third Republic decided to destroy the royal palace entirely. With its disappearance, the two long arms of the Louvre would henceforth open onto a magnificent perspective of the gardens of the Tuileries, the Place de la Concorde and the Arc de triomphe.

In 1981, François Mitterand decided to completely dedicate the Louvre to works of art: the Richelieu wing, occupied by the Ministry of Finance, would therefore become free. The architect Ieoh Ming Pei thus devised a project on a monumental scale, the pyramid in the middle of the Cour Napoléon being only the outward sign. On the inside, all of the collections would be redistributed throughout the renovated space. The largest museum in the world would henceforth be able to welcome its five million visitors per year.

# PLAN OF THE LOWER GROUND FLOOR

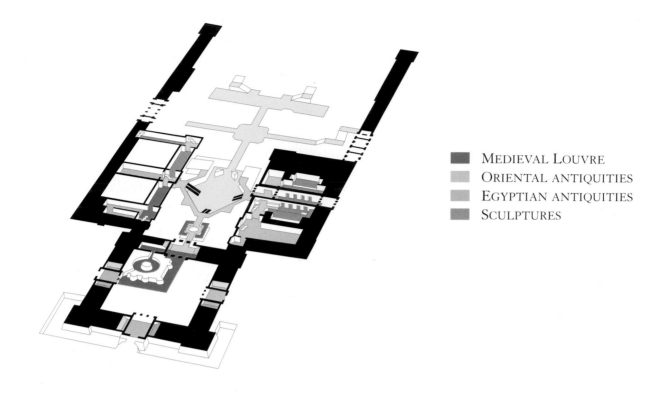

- ■ MEDIEVAL LOUVRE
- ■ ORIENTAL ANTIQUITIES
- ■ EGYPTIAN ANTIQUITIES
- ■ SCULPTURES

# PLAN OF THE GROUND FLOOR

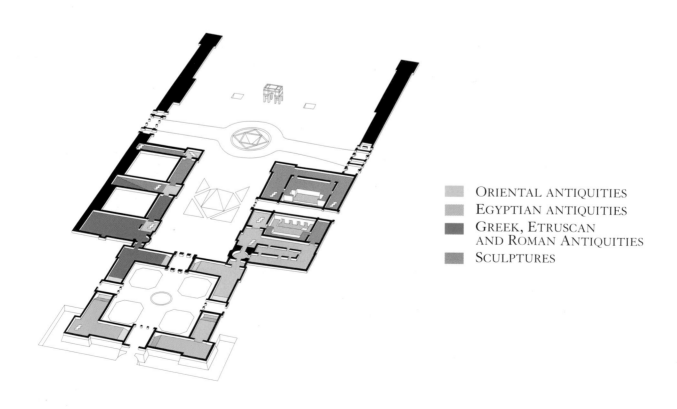

- ■ ORIENTAL ANTIQUITIES
- ■ EGYPTIAN ANTIQUITIES
- ■ GREEK, ETRUSCAN AND ROMAN ANTIQUITIES
- ■ SCULPTURES

# PLAN OF THE FIRST FLOOR

EGYPTIAN ANTIQUITIES
GREEK, ETRUSCAN
AND ROMAN ANTIQUITIES

PAINTINGS
GRAPHIC ARTS
OBJETS D'ART

# PLAN OF THE SECOND FLOOR

PAINTINGS
GRAPHIC ARTS

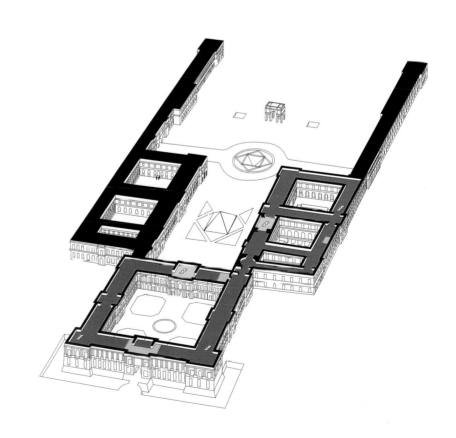

These works are situated
on the ground floor of the Richelieu wing,
in rooms 1b, 2 and 4.

1. *Intendant Ebih-Il*, Mari, circa 2400 BC, alabaster, eyes inlaid
   with shell and lapis lazuli, h: 52 cm
2. *Stela of Hammurabi*, Babylon, circa 1760 BC, black basalt, h: 225 cm
3. *Gudea holding a vessel from which water springs forth*, Telloh, dolerite,
   circa 2140 BC, h: 62 cm

## *Pious, warrior kings, who made justice reign*

**1** This statue served to immortalise Ebih-Il praying to his god. The inscription on the back reads: "Statue of Ebih-Il, intendant, devoted to the fecund Ishtar." Although the position of the intendant, seated on a wicker stool and wearing a *kaunakès*, a long skirt with wisps of sheeps wool, is rather conventional, his features are not without a certain realism.

**2** Hammurabi (1792-1750 BC), "Hammu the god is great", the most well known king of Babylon, is depicted at the top of the stela praying to Shamash, the sun god and god of justice. Following a prologue where the king is portrayed as a pious prince, assuring the happiness of his subjects, the code itself is a collection of 282 decrees of justice, based on 11 themes, dealing with family life as well as economic aspects. It is not strictly speaking a legal code, but rather a catalogue of judicial precedents in which the penalties vary according to the social origins of the victim.

3 "The day Ningirsu [the great god of Lagash] looked benevolently upon his town, his hand seized Gudea in the middle of the crowd, and he chose him as the leader of his people." King Gudea (which means "the chosen one", inferring: by his god) is always depicted in this attire: fine draping robes leaving one shoulder bare and a high-rimmed hat. His idealised features evoke strength and piety. He clutches to his chest a vessel from which four streams of water and fish spring forth, the cascading water evoking the four rivers irrigating the world: the Tigris, the Euphrates, the Nile and the Indus. An inscription dedicated to Geshtinanna, the goddess of life-giving water, is engraved on the front of his tunic.

# ORIENTAL
## ANTIQUITIES

These works are situated on the ground floor of the Richelieu wing, in rooms 4, 6 and 12.

1. *Frieze of archers*, Palace of Darius in Susa, circa 510 BC, enamelled bricks, h: 183 cm (archers)
2. *Horsemen of Assurbanipal*, 668-630 BC, gypseous alabaster, h: 129 cm
3. *Winged bull with human head,* Khorsabad, Iraq, courtyard of the palace of Sargon II, 713-706 BC, gypseous alabaster, h: 440 cm

## In the time of the great empires: the Assyrians and the Persians

**1** At the end of the 6th century BC, Darius made Susa capital of the Persian Empire. The frieze of archers decorated the walls of the palace. Carved in profile, with only the eye depicted face-on, they are thought to represent the ten thousand elite soldiers, known as the Immortals, who accompanied the king in his campaigns; or perhaps they simply represent the guards of the king's house.

**2** During the 7th century BC, Nineveh became the capital of Sargon II's successors. Assurbanipal, the last great king of Assyria, had many Mesopotamian texts copied for his library which contained up to twenty thousand tablets. His palace was decorated with reliefs recounting his military campaigns, together with hunting scenes.

**3** Dûr-Sharrukin, "fortress of Sargon", was the capital of the Assyrian kingdom, ruled by Sargon II. The side posts of the doors of his palace were composed of great beasts which were to be observed either face-on, motionless, or from the side, walking: this is why they have an extra front leg. These beasts were given the body of a bull, the breast of a lion, the wings of an eagle and a human head; they wore the horned tiara of the gods. By protecting the palace, these benevolent spirits ensured the stability of the Assyrian Kingdom. The texts between their legs describe the titles of Sargon, accounts of battles or the building of the palace, or curses against he who would destroy the works of the king. They were called *lamassu*, and those from Khorsabad are recognised by the daisies on the horned tiara.

# ORIENTAL
## ANTIQUITIES
### ISLAMIC ARTS

These works are situated on the lower ground floor of the Richelieu wing, in rooms 3, 4 and 8.

1. *Basin, known as the "Baptistery of Saint Louis"*, Syria or Egypt, end of the 13th-beginning of the 14th century, brass, silver and gold, h: 23 cm
2. *Pyxis of al-Mughira*, Cordoba, 968, ivory, h: 15 cm
3. *Bowl with a falconer on horseback*, Iran, beginning of the 13th century, ceramic, d: 22 cm

## From Spain to India, refined court art

Islam, "surrender to God", the religion founded in Arabia by the prophet Muhammad who died in 632, in little more than a century conquered a vast empire, spreading from Spain right up to India. The princes of this empire, both religious leaders and statesmen, commissioned works serving the Muslim faith, together with secular objects. The décor of the latter often described their favourite pastimes: music, banquets, dancing and hunting.

**1** Islamic craftsmen were skilled in metalwork. Dignitaries with the emblems of their office are displayed in the midst of an extremely dense animal and floral décor. Saint Louis was already dead when this basin was crafted. It was probably because it became part of the French royal collections that the basin was improperly given this name.

**2** Spain was conquered by the Muslims in 711, and Cordoba became the Moorish capital. The profuse décor of this box - sometimes described as a "fear of empty space" - is typical of Islamic art.

14

3

This bowl illustrates the theme of hunting. It demonstrates the technical virtuosity shown by the Islamic craftsmen very early on: for example, it was they who invented pottery six centuries before the West; they also developed a technique yielding extremely delicate colours, as in this case, by successive firing.

These works are situated on the first floor
of the Sully section, in rooms 21, 25 and 27,
and on the lower ground floor, in room 1.

1. *The goddess Hathor greets Seti I*, Valley of the Kings, circa 1300 BC, painted limestone, h: 226 cm
2. *Bust of Amenophis IV, known as Akhenaten*, Karnak, circa 1353-1337 BC, sandstone, h: 137 cm
3. *Sphinx*, Ancient Kingdom, Snefru (?), pink granite, h: 183 cm
4. *Stela of the Serpent King*, Abydos, circa 3100-2700 BC, limestone, h: 143 cm

## *Between the gods and man: the Pharaoh*

**1**

It was in the Valley of the Kings, to the west of Thebes, that most of the tombs of the kings of the New Kingdom were carved into the mountain. On the left, Hathor, "goddess of the western territory", i.e. of the dead, greets Seti I presenting him with his *menat* necklace, a symbol of rebirth. Their other hands are joined. The king, himself perceived as a god on this earth, stands face to face with the goddess. In order to please the gods, the Pharaoh gave them temples, images and statues; in exchange, the gods protected the land from catastrophe and chaos.

**2**

During the reign of Amenophis IV, the Egyptian gods were officially replaced by a single god, Aten, the solar disk. The Pharaoh then changed his name to Akhenaten, "servant of Aten", and decided to leave Thebes to establish the new capital dedicated to the new god on a new site, Akhetaten, the "horizon of the Aten", now Amarna. The effigy of the king adopted new aesthetic canons: an elongated face, a very long neck, almond-shaped eyes and highly defined lips.

**3** The sphinx - meaning "living image" - is a mythical beast with the body of a lion and a human head. It is the "living image" of the Pharaoh: it thus wears the *nemes*, the traditional head-dress of the pharaohs, and a false beard.

**4** Originally driven into the ground, this stela was found broken in the royal necropolis of Abydos. The king is symbolised by the hieroglyph of his name. This is carved above the palace architecture in which two narrow doors symbolising Northern and Southern Egypt may be distinguished. Standing firmly on the pharaoh's residence, the falcon personifies the god Horus, ancestor of the dynasty. A constant feature of Egyptian art already exists: the profile representation - the falcon - is associated with a front view - the eye.

# EGYPTIAN
## antiquities

These works are situated on the ground floor of the Sully wing, in rooms 14 and 17, and on the first floor: rooms 23 and 30.

1. *Funeral stela of Taperet*, circa 900-800 BC, painted wood, 31 x 29 cm
2. *Sarcophagus of Chancellor Imeneminet,* painted and stuccoed layered canvas, h: 188 cm
3. *Weighing the heart*, detail from the Nesmin papyrus, Late Period, 30th Dynasty (?)
4. *Funeral portrait of a young woman, known as "Portrait of Fayoum"*, Antinoë, painted wood, 2nd century AD (?), (Denon room A)
5. *Chancellor Nakhti*, Assiout, circa 2000 BC, acacia, h: 179 cm

## Life after death

"He who learns this book on earth or who has it written in his burial place will go out from his tomb on the days he chooses and will return without hindrance; he will be given bread, ale and meat from altar of Ra; he will receive land in the field of reeds where he will be given barley and wheat, and he will flourish as he did on earth" (*Book of the Dead*, chapter 1). The Egyptians believed in life after death for all, as long as they had led a just existence on earth. There, their life would resemble that which they had led here below, with the same needs and occupations. This is why different operations were carried out in order to preserve the body - embalming, and placing in the sarcophagus… - and also why the tombs contained everything the deceased would require, whether in the form of small models or images accompanied by magical formulas, the depiction of an object making it a reality.

2

After being embalmed, the body is wrapped in thin bandages and placed in several coffins which fit into each other.

1

According to legend, during a battle in which Horus wished to avenge his father Osiris, Seth tore out the eye of Horus. However, Thoth miraculously returned the eye to Horus. He thus became the prototype of physical integrity. This is why he is often portrayed on the coffins: he thus guarantees the dead the full use of their body.

**3** The god Osiris sits enthroned in the hall of justice. On the right, the deceased, Nesmin, guided by Maat; in the middle, on one side of the scales, is the heart of the deceased; Horus and Anubis supervise the weighing, while Thoth, "master of the words of the god", serves as a clerk. If the heart of the deceased is heavy with sin, it will be devoured; but if it is as light as a feather, the deceased will be taken before Osiris who will assign him his place in the beyond.

**5** This statue of Nakhti was found in a recess of his tomb with his sarcophagus and several small models.

**4** The personalised funeral portrait, placed over the face of the mummy, appeared late in Egypt during Roman occupation.

# EGYPTIAN
## antiquities

These works are situated
on the first floor of the Sully section,
in rooms 6 and 22.

1. *Stela of Nefertiabet*, Giza,
   circa 2620-2500 BC,
   painted limestone, h: 38 cm
2. Writing tools
3. *Seated scribe*, Saqqara,
   2620-2500 BC,
   painted limestone, h: 53 cm

## *Egyptian writing*

Egyptian writing consisted of hiero-glyphs. Having long been a mystery, it was Champollion who, in 1822, first realised that they were made up of pho-netic signs and pictograms.

The elegant Nefertiabet, sister or daughter of Kheops, dressed in feline-print robes, is seated on a stool with the legs of a bull before her offering table. The hieroglyphs indicate her title, the list of materials given to her to embalm her body, the list of food she will need for the beyond - bread, ale, beef, poultry - together with the list of unguents.

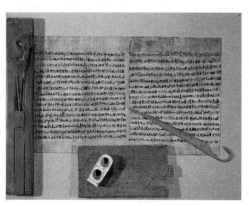

A scribe's equipment consisted of several instruments: a palette with wells, brushes made from reeds, and pigment cakes (mineral pigments crushed and formed into cakes using a binding agent), a box containing rolls of papyrus, papyrus-cutters to straighten the edges of the sheets, smoothing tools to "smooth" the sheets, and seals.

Everything suggests that this high-ranking civil servant, who remains anonymous, listened to his superior's dictation: his attentive expression, his thin lips, his clenched jaw and deep gaze - a rock crystal cone has been inlaid in the eye. Ready to commence writing, his left hand holds the papyrus which will unfurl as he writes.

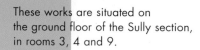

# EGYPTIAN
## antiquities

These works are situated on
the ground floor of the Sully section,
in rooms 3, 4 and 9.

1. *Hunting with nets, detail of a wall of the Mastaba
   of Akhethetep*, Saqqara, circa 2400 BC, limestone
2. *Model of a small boat, sailing scene*, Egypt during
   the Middle Kingdom, polychrome wood, 38.5 x 81 cm
3. *Cosmetic spoon in the shape of a swimmer*,
   circa 1400 BC, tamarisk and boxwood, l: 33 cm
4. *Hippopotamus*, circa 2000-1900 BC,
   Egyptian "pottery", h: 12.7 cm
5. *Woman carrying a platter*, circa 1950 BC,
   painted and stuccoed ficus, h: 108 cm

## *A day in the life of the Egyptians*

Paintings and objects recovered from tombs have enabled
us to discover the day-to-day life of the Egyptians.

**1** The Pharaoh, who had exclusive possession of the land of Egypt, allocated prop-
erty to his courtiers by royal favour. Akhethetep was one such courtier. Captivating
scenes of life on his lands are depicted on the walls of his mastaba ("bench" in Arabic,
i.e. the construction situated above his tomb). In this detail, it can be seen how the
Egyptians used large nets to capture birds which they would then fatten.

**2**

The life of the Egyptians was punctuated by the yearly flooding of the Nile, this "nourishing river, giver of blessings, which creates all that is good", according to one of their hymns. The river then covered an area which varied according to the flooding and thus made it possible to cultivate land which would otherwise have remained arid.

**3**

Perfumes and cosmetics came to enrich the finery of Egyptians in noble society. The cavity of this cosmetic spoon is hidden beneath the pivoting wings of the duck.

**4**

The Egyptians hunted the hippopotamus in the swamps of the Delta. Placed in the tombs, these hippopotamuses represented the evil and the dangers of the swamp which the deceased had to cross. The motifs painted on its body portray the plants growing in the waters of the swamp.

**5**

This elegant willowy figure, remarkable in terms of its size, carries a leg of beef on her platter and a water bottle in her right hand. She thus provides the deceased with eternal nourishment.

These works are situated
in the Denon wing, in room 1,
and in the Sully section
on the ground floor, in room 7.

1. Euphronius, *Crater of Herakles and Antaeus*, circa 510 BC, h: 45 cm
2. *Corè of Samos*, Sanctuary of Hera, circa 560 BC, marble, h: 192 cm
3. *Plaque of the Ergastines* (detail), fragment of the frieze of the Panathenaea, Temple of the Parthenon, Athens, circa 430 BC, marble, h: 96 cm
4. *Head of a horseman, known as "Rampin the Horseman"*, Athens, circa 550 BC, marble, h: 29 cm

## The first marble-cutters in the Age of Pericles

**1**

Like on other vases, Euphronius signed this chalice-type crater with red figures. This artist of genius, extremely gifted in his portrayal of the male anatomy, was fond of large vases which gave the depicted scenes a monumental scale.

**2**

Although the name of the sculptor who executed this *ex voto* is not known, its commissioner is revealed by the inscription: "I was dedicated to Hera as an offering by Chéramyes." At that time, wealthy families decorated sanctuaries with statues, either of young men (*couros*, meaning young man in Greek), or young girls (*corè*, in Greek).

**3**

When Pericles decided to rebuild the temple of Athena situated on the Acropolis - which would become the Parthenon, he entrusted the work to Phidias who created the décor to the glory of the Athenian city. A large frieze ran along the outside wall of the temple, illustrating the Great Panathenaea, the major feast celebrated by Athenians in honour of Athena, the goddess and protector of their city. The Ergastines, depicted here, were young girls from the important families of the city who had been chosen to weave the sacred tunic to be presented to the goddess in a procession.

4 Only the head of this horseman, which was found on the Acropolis, is authentic: the body and mount are taken from moulds of the originals preserved at the Museum of Athens. A second horseman, symmetrical in position in relation to the latter, was also found at the same site. The two horsemen thus formed a group: the men faced each other whereas the horses' heads were turned to the outside. Although the identity of the men is not known, this *ex voto* was, in fact, installed in the open air on the Acropolis of Athens: a hole on the top of the horse-man's head was intended to hold a small bronze disk placed over the statues to protect them from birds.

These works are situated
on the first floor
of the Denon wing,
and on the landing.

1. *Venus de Milo*, Melos, circa 100 BC, marble, h: 202 cm (Sully, room 12)
2. *Victory of Samothrace*, circa 190 BC, marble, h: 328 cm

## *The spread of classicism*

**1**

This unmissable feature of the
Louvre was discovered in two
pieces on Melos, an island in the
Cyclades. This *Venus*, which has
become the symbol of classical art
for the general public, is in fact a
late variant of the theme created in
the 4th century BC by Praxiteles in
the *Bare Aphrodite*, which runs
through Hellenistic art.

**2**

This Victory, represented in the form of a
winged goddess placed on the prow of a war-
ship, undoubtedly commemorated a naval
victory. The sculpture was discovered in 1863
on a hill, from which it dominated a sanctuary. It is colossal in size in relation to the prow;
there was once a block of marble between the
statue and the prow, on which the sculptor's
signature could be seen. Gusts of wind lift the
layered draping robes; in places, the wet fabric
clings to her body revealing her form. The
strength, vigour and breath which bring this
Victory to life have turned it into a sculptural
masterpiece.

# ANTIQUITIES

These works are situated
on the ground floor
of the Denon wing,
in rooms 18, 24 and 29.

1. *Portrait of Livia*, circa 31 BC, basalt, h: 34 cm
2. *Phoenix mosaic*, Antioch, 6th century, h: 600 cm
3. *Sarcophagus of a married couple*, Cerveteri, 530-510 BC,
   polychrome terracotta, h: 111 cm

## From the Etruscans to the Romans

**1**

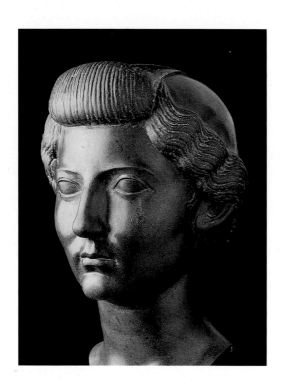

Portraiture was really a Roman speciality explained by the development of the cult of the emperor. Originally reserved for the patricians, portraiture, either full-length or busts, was then extended to the wealthy plebeians. The *Portrait of Livia* was fashioned in basalt: it is therefore thought that it was executed in Egypt, during the decisive Battle of Actium in 31 BC, when Octavian, the future Augustus and husband of Livia, defeated the fleet commanded by Mark Antony and Cleopatra. It is an idealised portrait: with the advent of the Empire in 27 BC, portraits of the emperor and his family invaded the public sphere. Livia's hairstyle, with the rolled lock of hair at the front, would be copied not only by all the women in the imperial family, but also in private portrayals.

**2**

Like portraiture, mosaic is an art form that was extensively developed by the Romans: mosaics adorned the floors and walls of their homes, and fountains, etc. This mosaic belonged to the genre of carpet mosaics: at the centre, a phoenix stands out on a background strewn with small roses; like on a carpet, a border - in this case, ibexes of which only the forequarters are depicted - surrounds the mosaic.

3   This sarcophagus, discovered in a tomb with chambers beneath a burial
mound, typical of Etruscan tombs, is in actual fact a funeral urn in the form
of a banqueting table, the cover of which depicts a loving couple lying side
by side. It is a banquet scene; the wife held a perfume jar from which she
poured a few drops into her husband's left hand (missing). Perfume was part
of the funeral ritual, as was wine, also depicted here by the wineskins
beneath their elbows.

These works are situated
on the second floor of the Richelieu wing,
in rooms 1, 3 and 4.

1. Jean Malouel, *Large Round Pietà*, circa 1400, tempera on wood, d: 64.5 cm
2. French Painter, *Portrait of Jean II Le Bon*, circa 1350, tempera on wood, 59.8 x 44.6 cm
3. Enguerrand Quarton, *Pietà of Villeneuve-lès-Avignon*, circa 1455, tempera on wood, 163 x 218 cm

## *The beginnings of easel painting*

**1** This *Pietà* was painted for one of the sons of Jean II *Le Bon*, Philippe *Le Hardi*, whose coats of arms are shown on the back of the painting. Here, the theme of the Trinity - it is God the Father who holds Christ - is associated with that of the *Pietà*. Philippe *Le Hardi*, who was a great patron like his father and brothers (King Charles V, Jean de Berry, Duke Louis d'Anjou), had a special devotion for the Trinity: the Carthusian Monastery of Champmol, near Dijon, which he had built to serve as his family burial site, was placed under his patronage.

**2** This painting is the oldest surviving easel portrait and one of the first known individual portraits. Until then, artists painted portraits of donors within a group whereas, here, the individual has been painted on his own. The profile portrayal is probably related to the royal effigies depicted on medals. Since Jean does not wear a crown, it is assumed that this panel was painted while he was still only the Duke of Normandy. The inscription *"jehan roy de France"* would have been added at a later date.

3 The *Pietà* in which the Virgin Mary holds her dead son on her knee became the favourite theme for artists at the end of the Middle Ages. The words of the brief inscription on the edge of the painting: "All you who pass by, look around and see if there is any suffering like that inflicted on me", a sentence taken from Jeremiah's Lamentations (1, 12), were probably on the lips of the Virgin.

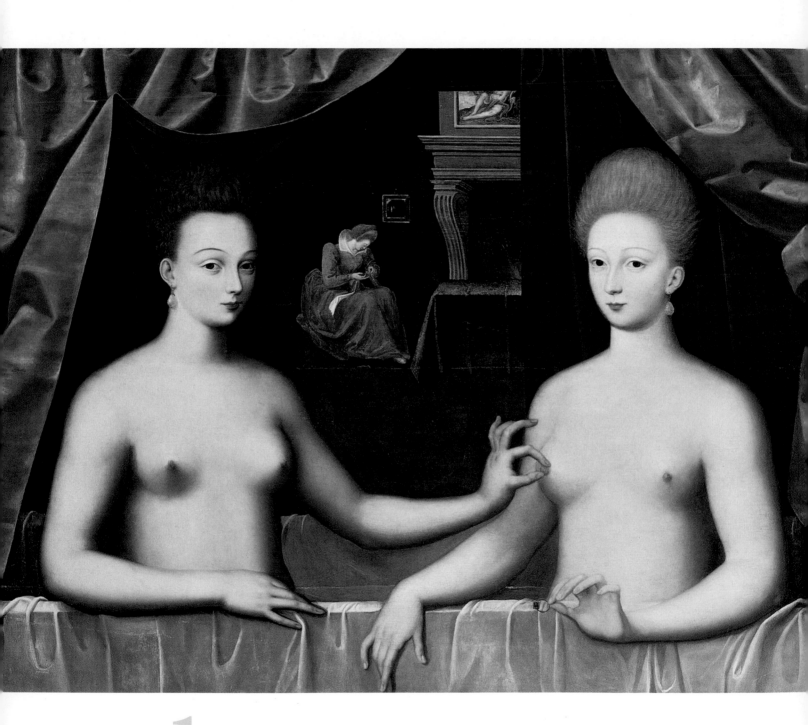

**1** Gabrielle d'Estrées, mistress of Henri IV, on the right in her bath, is probably accompanied by her sister, the Duchess de Villars. The latter holds Gabrielle d'Estrées' nipple: this coded gesture alludes to the birth of the Duke de Vendôme, in 1594, the fruit of the love affair between the king and his mistress. Gabrielle d'Estrées holds a ring in her left hand, a token of their love.

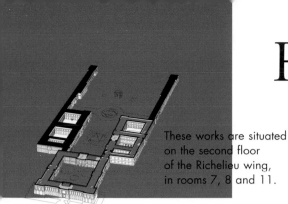

# FRENCH
## PAINTINGS

These works are situated
on the second floor
of the Richelieu wing,
in rooms 7, 8 and 11.

1. Fontainebleau School, *Gabrielle d'Estrées and One of Her Sisters Bathing*, circa 1595, oil on wood, 96 x 125 cm
2. Fontainebleau School, *Diana the Huntress*, circa 1550, oil on canvas, 191 x 132 cm
3. Attributed to Jean and François Clouet, *François I, King of France*, circa 1530, oil on wood, 96 x 74 cm

## *Portraiture in all its shapes and forms*

The idealised portrait of kings and princes, but also sensual, naked women, was a subject much favoured by painters working at the Château de Fontainebleau for François I, and then for his successors throughout the 16th century.

Diane de Poitiers, mistress of Henri II, is portrayed with the attributes of Diana the Huntress. During the Renaissance, artists painted portraits of the important figures of this world in the guise of mythological beings, which was a way of glorifying kings and aristocrats, but also served as a pretext to paint nudes in total legitimacy. The idealised nude adopted Mannerist values: the head tends to be small in relation to the rest of the body, while the silhouette unfurls in an arabesque.

Jean Clouet and his son François were great drawers: at Court, portraits they had drawn were passed round and the game consisted in identifying the subject. Although the crowns in the background, the medal of the Order of Saint Michael and sword are the marks of royal power, the attire of an Italian gentleman and the gloves, an aristocratic emblem, evoke the enlightened prince, François I.

These works are situated
on the second floor
of the Sully section,
in rooms 28 and 29.

# FRENCH
## PAINTINGS

1. Georges de La Tour, *The Cheat*, circa 1635, oil on canvas, 106 x 146 cm
2. Louis or Antoine Le Nain, *Peasant Family in an Interior*, circa 1640, oil on canvas, 113 x 159 cm
3. Georges de La Tour, *Mary Magdalene by a Night-Light*, circa 1640-1645, oil on canvas, 128 x 94 cm

## *Reality transformed by the light*

A life still enshrouded in mystery, forty or so attributed works, endlessly repeated themes, innumerable copies and forgotten for over two centuries: this is how Georges de La Tour is perceived today. The painter lived in the time of Louis XIII, in the Lorraine region then ravaged by wars and epidemics. Moreover, the little that is known of the nature of this baker's son is hardly in keeping with the profoundly human, silent atmosphere conveyed by his paintings: surviving documents in fact describe him as arrogant, greedy and violent.

1

The interplay of hands and glances silently develops the cheating between the courtesan and her friend, in collusion with the servant. "Love, wine and gambling have lost more than one man," said a famous proverb of the time. La Tour had thus not forgotten anything.

**2**

Mainly known for their paintings of country folk, the three La Nain brothers also executed "large history paintings". Since they simply signed their paintings "Le Nain", it is difficult to ascribe to each artist that which is due to him.

**3**

Four versions of this theme have been preserved, not including the numerous copies. The face of Saint Mary Magdalene still appears in profile, lit by the tall flame of a candle. Next to her are two closed books, a crucifix and a rope with which to chastise herself. After a life of sin, the saint, having become a hermit, contemplates her life, and also death: the skull on her lap at the centre of the painting evokes passing time and the vanity of earthly things, just like the burning candle. The extreme stylisation of the forms bathed in the golden light suggests contemplation.

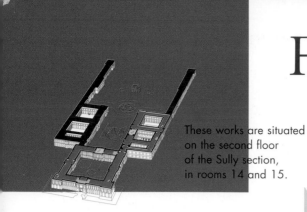

These works are situated
on the second floor
of the Sully section,
in rooms 14 and 15.

# FRENCH
## PAINTINGS

1. Claude Gellée, known as Le Lorrain, *Cleopatra Disembarking at Tarsus*, 1642-1643, oil on canvas, 119 x 170 cm
2. Nicolas Poussin, *The Rape of the Sabine Women*, 1637-1638, oil on canvas, 159 x 206 cm
3. Nicolas Poussin, *Portrait of the Artist*, 1650, oil on canvas, 98 x 74 cm

## *Two expatriates in Rome*

Many of the most outstanding French paintings during the 17<sup>th</sup> century were produced in Rome. Nicolas Poussin, "the most Roman of the French painters", and Claude Gellée, known as Le Lorrain, spent almost their entire working life in the Eternal City. In this sense, they belonged to the Roman world, even though they would have a major influence on the history of French painting.

1

"Another time, Poussin, Claude Gellée and I rode to Tivoli to paint and draw land-scapes from life," reminisced the painter Joachim von Sandrart in his history of art. However, make no mistake: although Le Lorrain occasionally borrows a motif which has been actually observed, his landscapes are re-composed to give an ideal image of nature, the real subject of his paintings.

**2** Here, Poussin portrays an episode from the beginnings of Roman history: after having founded the city of Rome, Romulus invited the populations in the neighbouring cities to take part in the games. The invitation was, in fact, part of a cunning plan: when the signal was given, the men seized the young Sabine women to take them as wives. The movement and agitation, the facial expressions and the composition make it possible to read the painting like a book, which was the desire of Poussin himself.

**3** Poussin gave in to the entreaties of two of his friends and painted two self-portraits in total. No other portraits are known to have been painted by him: like many of his contemporaries, he considered this a minor genre in relation to history painting. Poussin portrays himself as a painter: his right hand holds a portfolio, while his torso stands out on a series of framed canvases.

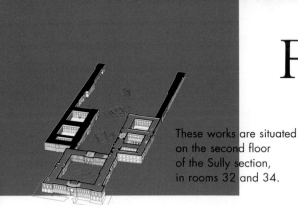

# FRENCH
## PAINTINGS

These works are situated on the second floor of the Sully section, in rooms 32 and 34.

1. Charles Le Brun, *Chancellor Séguier*, circa 1657-1661, oil on canvas, 295 x 357 cm
2. Nicolas de Largillière, *Charles Le Brun, Chief Painter to the King*, 1683-1686, oil on canvas, 232 x 187 cm
3. Hyacinthe Rigaud, *Louis XIV, King of France*, 1701, oil on canvas, 277 x 194 cm

## *Art in the service of the greatest of kings*

**1** Chancellor Séguier was Le Brun's first patron. This majestic equestrian portrait is perfectly put together: the horse is depicted strictly in profile, whereas the pages are arranged in a frieze.

**2** When artists were admitted to the Academy, they had to paint an "entry piece". Largillière decided to flatter the director of the Academy, Charles Le Brun, by choosing to portray him as his subject. Even though he himself was a painter, Le Brun is mainly remembered as the chief organiser of the arts during the reign of Louis XIV, arts that were to serve the greatness and glory of the king, and therefore France. Until the death of Colbert in 1683, Le Brun would be chief painter to the king, but also director of the royal works (Les Gobelins and La Savonnerie), and director of the all-powerful French Royal Academy of Painting and Sculpture. He thus supervised all the major work at the different royal residences - Versailles, of course, but also Marly, Meudon and Trianon. The title "dictator of the arts", by which he was sometimes known, is probably well founded.

3  Painted as a gift for Philippe V, grandson of Louis XIV and King of Spain, the Sun King was so pleased with this portrait that he finally decided to keep it for himself. The monarch, then aged sixty-three, is depicted dressed in his coronation robes with the emblems of his power. Rigaud and Largillière were the two great portraitists at the end of the reign of Louis XIV.

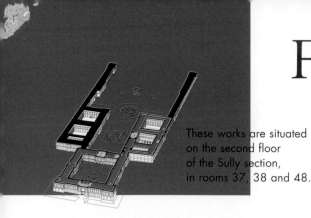

These works are situated
on the second floor
of the Sully section,
in rooms 37, 38 and 48.

# FRENCH
## PAINTINGS

1. François Boucher, *Diana Bathing*, Paris, 1743, oil on canvas, 57 x 73 cm
2. Élisabeth-Louise Vigée-Lebrun, *Mme Vigée-Lebrun and Daughter*, 1789, oil on canvas, 130 x 94 cm (Denon, room 75)
3. Jean-Honoré Fragonard, *The Bolt*, circa 1778, oil on canvas, 73 x 93 cm
4. Jean-Antoine Watteau, *Pilgrimage to the Island of Cythera*, 1717, oil on canvas, 129 x 194 cm

## *Mystery, lightness and virtuosity*

**1**

In Boucher's work, the mythological subject is usually an excuse to paint suggestive nudes: the gods thus lose their heroic features for a more sensual and erotic image. These romantic mythological scenes achieved great success at the time: Boucher would become the favourite painter of Louis XV and Mme de Pompadour.

**2**

Marie-Antoinette's portraitist was forced to leave France for political reasons. Extremely famous in her time, she travelled the whole of Europe painting portraits of the aristocracy. She depicts herself here holding her little daughter with natural, delicate tenderness.

**3**

Fragonard's brushstroke, often extremely free and rapid as seen in his half-length portraits, is much more precise and fine in this painting with its slightly roguish subject.

4   For his entry piece on admittance to the Academy, Watteau produced a painting which did not fit into any of the categories defined by the Academy: the genre known as *"fête galante"* was therefore created for the piece. This painting gave rise to considerable debate as to meaning of the scene depicted: are the lovers on their way to the Island of Venus, or are they melancholic and weary as they prepare to leave the enchanted island? Is it a cheerful departure towards the ecstasies of Cythera, or an elegy to the fleetingness of love which is inevitably eroded by time? The figures, many seen from behind, stand out on a hazy background which gives the composition a melancholic, mysterious air.

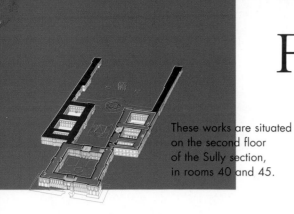

These works are situated
on the second floor
of the Sully section,
in rooms 40 and 45.

# FRENCH
## PAINTINGS

1. Jean-Siméon Chardin, *Self-portrait at the Easel*, circa 1776, pastel, 40.7 x 32.5 cm
2. Jean-Siméon Chardin, *Child with a Teetotum*, circa 1738, oil on canvas, 67 x 76 cm
3. Jean-Siméon Chardin, *The Jar of Olives*, 1760, oil on canvas, 71 x 98 cm

## *Everyday life as the subject*

**2** In this particular piece, Chardin is half-way between the portrait and the genre scene. Like in several of his paintings of children, the young boy, depicted in this half-length portrait, is concentrating hard and engrossed in his game, with no care for the outside world. The silent life of simple childhood games.

**3**

**1** At the end of his life, the eyesight of the painter known as *"bonhomme Chardin"* began to fail, and he abandoned oils for pastels. He then executed portraits which were extremely bold but true, as is the case of this self-portrait painted three years before his death: he was aged seventy-seven.

"There were several small paintings by Chardin at the Salon. Nearly all of them were of fruit and dining implements. It was life itself. The objects loom out of the canvas and are so life-like that they deceive the eyes. The one that can be seen when climbing the stairs particularly deserves attention… If I intended my child to become a painter, I would surely purchase this one piece. "Copy it for me," I would say, "copy it again"… because the porcelain bowl is actually made of porcelain; because the olives are, in fact, separated from our gaze by the water in which they float; because we simply have to take these biscuits and eat them; this Seville orange, cut it open and squeeze it; drink the glass of wine; peel the fruits; place the knife in the pâté… Oh Chardin, you do not grind white, red or black on your palette, but rather the very substance of objects; you place air and light on the tip of your paintbrush and fix them onto the canvas" (Diderot, comments on the Salon of 1763).

These works are situated
on the first floor
of the Denon wing,
in rooms 75 and 77.

# FRENCH
## PAINTINGS

1. Eugène Delacroix, *The Death of Sardanapalus*, 1827-1828, oil on canvas, 392 x 496 cm
2. Jacques-Louis David, *The Coronation of Napoleon 1*, 1806-1807, oil on canvas, 621 x 979 cm

## *New heroes*

**1** The tale of Sardanapalus has been told by many writers: when the king of Babylon heard he had lost the battle, he decided to perish with his own people rather than give himself up to his enemies. Delacroix chose to portray the death of the horses and the king's mistresses. The profusion of strong colours, the contorted forms, the extremely dense composition, and oriental theme made it a manifesto of the Romantic aesthetic. This piece, exhibited at the Salon of 1828, provoked radically opposed reactions: while some described Delacroix as "possessed" or an "intoxicated savage", Victor Hugo exclaimed: "Sardanapalus is a magnificent, immense thing".

2 "What depth, what truth! This is not art, we can step into your painting," Napoleon is said to have exclaimed when he saw this immense canvas which took David two years to complete. Two hundred dignitaries, some of whom are perfectly recognisable, are present as Napoleon gets ready to place the crown on Josephine's head. David even depicted certain absentees, the most famous being Madame, the Emperor's mother. After having glorified the heroes of antiquity in his canvases, David found himself a new contemporary hero: Napoleon.

1 This was still an acutely topical subject when Delacroix decided to paint this historical piece in which he commemorates the *Trois Glorieuses*, the three days of the revolution of July 1830 which ended the reign of Charles X. However, Delacroix adds mythical inspiration to the historical reality of the violent battles by portraying the figure of a marching Liberty: larger than the others, her bare bosom inevitably evokes the allegory of Victory. Although the piece received a great deal of attention at the Salon, it had a mixed reception: Liberty was described as "vulgar" and the painter was criticised for having defended the "riffraff".

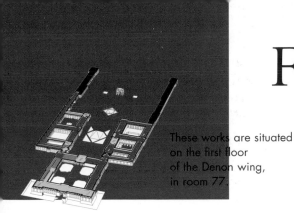

These works are situated
on the first floor
of the Denon wing,
in room 77.

# FRENCH
## PAINTINGS

1. Eugène Delacroix, *Liberty Guiding the People*, 1830, oil on canvas, 260 x 325 cm
2. Théodore Géricault, *The Raft of the Medusa*, 1819, oil on canvas, 491 x 716 cm
3. Théodore Géricault, *Madwoman Obsessed with Gambling*, 1822, oil on canvas, 77 x 64 cm

## *Topical themes in painting*

**2**

In 1816, a French frigate ran aground off Senegal. The officers thus built a makeshift raft which would soon become packed with one hundred and fifty castaways. Provisions quickly became sparse, and only fifteen people would survive the nightmarish ordeal. By suggesting the negligence of the Medusa's captain, an expatriate who had been reinstated in the Royal Navy by special favour despite not having sailed since the age of twenty-five, it was said that Géricault wanted to cast discredit on the government of the Restoration. The morbid realism of the bodies also shocked members of the general public. Géricault had obtained parts of corpses: arms, torsos and legs from the Hôpital Beaujon nearby.

**3**

A friend of the painter, Dr Georget, who specialised in insanity, urged Géricault to paint a series of half-length portraits illustrating various types of mental illness. The painter took care to avoid portraying madness in its grotesque or comical forms. Instead, with great freedom in his brushstrokes, he soberly and aptly rendered the closed world of these patients whose extreme sensitivity can be glimpsed on their faces.

# FRENCH
## PAINTINGS

These works are situated on the second floor of the Sully section, in rooms 60 and 63, and on the first floor of the Denon wing, in room 75.

1. Jean-Auguste-Dominique Ingres, *The Valpinçon Bather*, 1808, oil on canvas, 146 x 97 cm
2. Jean-Auguste-Dominique Ingres, *The Large Odalisque*, 1814, oil on canvas, 91 x 162 cm
3. Hippolyte Flandrin, *Naked Young Man Sitting by the Sea*, 1836, oil on canvas, 98 x 124 cm

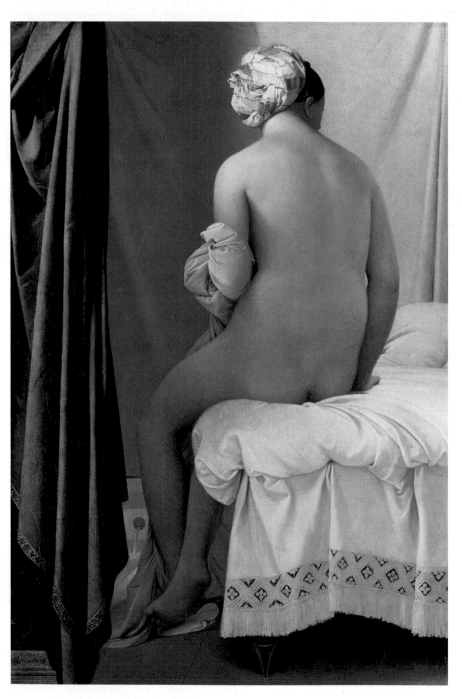

## *Drawing and exoticism*

**1**

*The Valpinçon Bather*, like *The Large Odalisque*, was painted while Ingres was in Italy. Seated on the edge of a bed, neither her face nor hands can be seen. As is often the case in his work, the nude is almost stylised: the neck and shoulders do not accurately correspond to the rules of anatomy, but the perfect curves, in modulated, balanced light, evoke a sensual world with great subtlety. The same figure is seen again in a much later work, *The Turkish Bath*, this time sitting on the floor and holding a musical instrument.

2 After the Napoleonic campaigns, the Orient became fashionable, among painters and writers - *Les Orientales* by Hugo only needs to spring to mind. Many travelled: Delacroix to Morocco, Byron to Greece… and Ingres could not escape the trend. Here, the fan of peacock feathers, the hookah, the shimmering turban and the very theme of the odalisque give the piece an oriental mood. The nude particularly emphasises line: it is the beauty of the line which creates the beauty of the body. It does not matter that the drawing did not scrupulously respect the rules of anatomy - Ingres' critics maintained that the odalisque had too many vertebrae.

3

"Please tell M. Ingres that he, Raphael and Phidias are the only persons with whom I discuss painting," Flandrin wrote to his brother. Ingres' faithful pupil effectively illustrates the supremacy of drawing. A strong liking for academic proportions is also seen in his work: a pure line begins at the head, draws the contours of the body, continuing along the legs down to the toes pointing towards the sea.

# FRENCH
## PAINTINGS

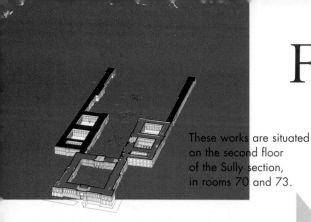

These works are situated on the second floor of the Sully section, in rooms 70 and 73.

## Jean-Baptiste Corot

1. Jean-Baptiste Corot, *The Lady in Blue*, 1874, oil on canvas, 80 x 50.5 cm
2. Jean-Baptiste Corot, *The Bridge of Narni*, 1826, oil on canvas, 34 x 48 cm
3. Jean-Baptiste Corot, *Memory of Mortefontaine*, 1864, oil on canvas, 65 x 89 cm

**1**

"He painted trees better than anyone, and was even better with his figures," affirmed Degas. However, Corot's contemporaries essentially perceived him as a landscape painter, and ignored the fact that he had painted figures all his life and was particularly fond of young women at the end of his career. The gaze of *The Lady in Blue*, painted a year before his death, seems a little lost: who, or what, is she looking at? "The artist made his creations in his own image: gentle, tender dreamers, taken up with flowers and music," affirmed Moreau-Nélaton, a great connoisseur and major collector of the work of a painter who was known by other painters as *"papa Corot"* due to his great kindness.

Corot continually alternated work from life with work in the studio. This landscape belongs to his studies taken from life while staying in Italy as a young artist. He then used them to re-compose paintings in his studio, sometimes several years later. These studies aimed to preserve what Corot referred to as "the first impression": he did not therefore consider them finished pieces. It was the general public's fondness for sketches which caused these preparatory paintings to be interpreted as innovative pieces heralding the Impressionist aesthetic.

**2**

3 This landscape, painted in the artist's prime, illustrates the misty and dream-like atmosphere which swept through Corot's landscapes from 1850 onwards. His brushstroke became vibrant and light (which some criticised him for), the atmosphere hazy, and the figures slightly blurred: "the fog needs time to lift". The canvas would be covered with a fairly limited range of colours, from the blues of the sky and water to the browns and greens of the vegetation.

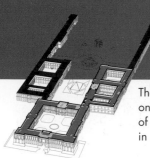

These works are situated
on the second floor
of the Richelieu wing,
in rooms 4 and 5.

1. Rogier van der Weyden, *The Annunciation*, circa 1435,
   oil on wood, 86 x 93 cm
2. Hans Memling, *Angel Holding an Olive Branch*, circa 1480,
   oil on wood, 16.4 x 11 cm
3. Jan van Eyck, *Chancellor Rolin's Virgin*, circa 1434,
   paint on wood, 66 x 62 cm

## *The "Flemish Primitives"*

**1** Painted at the beginning of van der Weyden's career,
*The Annunciation*, which portrays the Virgin in the privacy
of her room, already demonstrates the artist's virtuosity in
the rendering of the objects moulded by soft light, as
shown by the shadow of the transparent flask or candle-
holder on the mantelpiece.

**2** At the end of the Middle Ages, wealthy,
high-ranking individuals sometimes obtained permission from the Pope to cele-
brate the Eucharist at home on portable
altars which were probably decorated with
small triptychs. Memling's *Angel* was
undoubtedly one such devotional painting.

3

The Virgin holding the Child, about to be crowned by an angel, appears as if in a vision to Nicolas Rolin, Chancellor of the Duke of Burgundy, Philippe *Le Bon*. The meticulous realism in the work of van Eyck, official painter to the duke, makes every aspect of the piece present and alive: the tiles are cold, the fabric of the chancellor's gold brocade cloak is slightly stiff, the wrinkled skin on his neck sags somewhat and the veins at his temples pulsate. The light moulds the space and the forms. It restores the substance to things. However, this realism must not detract since the material reality, painted so painstakingly, serves to illustrate the spiritual meaning of the painting. For example, the flowers depicted in the small enclosed garden are references to the Virgin and Christ: the lily symbolises the Virgin's chastity and virginity and the daisies, her humility… Here, everything has a meaning, every detail counts. Contrary to what has long been maintained, it was not van Eyck who invented oil paint with its numerous advantages: saturation and brilliance of colour, blended brushstrokes… However, he developed a mixture that has not yet been identified but which enabled the oil to dry more rapidly, allowing the painter to superimpose lightly coloured layers - glazes - which give the pieces painted by the "Flemish primitives" this smooth, enamelled appearance.

# NORTHERN
## PAINTINGS

These works are situated
on the second floor
of the Richelieu wing,
in rooms 5, 9 and 10.

1. Hieronymus Bosch, *The Ship of Fools*, beginning of the 16th century, oil on wood, 58 x 32.5 cm
2. Pieter Bruegel, the Elder, *The Beggars*, 1568, oil on wood, 18 x 21 cm
3. Quentin Metsys, *The Money-Lender and His Wife*, 1514, oil on wood, 70.5 x 67 cm

## *Realism and morality*

2

The portrayal of the five cripples, with fox or marten tails pinned to their clothing, is difficult to interpret: whether a political or social satirical attack or a parody of the Twelfth Night, the piece has still not revealed all its secrets.

3

1

Bosch was not the only one interested in madness: in 1494, Sebastian Brant published a work also entitled *The Ship of Fools*, in which he satirised the vices and shortcomings of a corrupt society, which probably inspired Bosch; *The Praise of Folie* by Erasmus, in which the author criticised the different social classes, particularly the clergy, was published in 1509.

According to van Mander, "Art arrived at Anvers closely on the heels of wealth". In fact, it was from the 16th century onwards that Anvers gradually supplanted the city of Bruges to become an international trade centre with a flourishing art market. Numerous painters moved there, including Quentin Metsys who, in this piece, depicts a money-lender and his wife in their shop, sitting next to each other on a bench, in front of

shelves holding a number of objects. Like the Flemish painters of the previous century, Quentin Metsys describes them in an analytical fashion, pushing *trompe-l'œil* painting to its limits: the light reflecting on the bottle or on the pearls, the grain of the materials and the landscape reflected in the mirror are wonderfully handled. None of the objects were chosen by chance. The mirror between the two figures and the snuffed candle on the shelf serve as a reminder to the fact that life passes by and that one should not become attached to material values - the pieces of gold and pearls depicted here. The scales allude to the weighing of souls at the Last Judgement. The woman holds a religious book which falls open onto an image of the Virgin: the one able to intervene on behalf of sinners at the Last Judgement.

**1**

In 1622, Marie de' Medici, Queen of France and widow of Henri IV (who was assassinated in 1610), called on the Flemish artist Rubens to paint "episodes from the illustrious life and heroic deeds" of the queen and her Regency. This series of twenty-four paintings was to adorn a gallery in the newly built Palais du Luxembourg. The contract specified that Rubens was to paint this series himself - representing almost three hundred square metres of painting to be completed in under three years! The project was highly original since it relates the life of a historical figure, Marie de' Medici, no longer through a set of complex allegories or mythological tales, but in a narrative and epic way: each scene illustrates an event taken from the life of the queen, who appears as an idealised "heroine" protected by the gods. The artist, then renowned throughout Europe, brings together the characteristics of the baroque style: the extremely clear composition, depth of space, dynamic scenes, and refined shades obtained using layered glazes which give the flesh tones their legendary transparency.

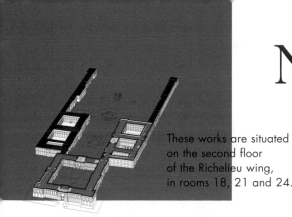

These works are situated
on the second floor
of the Richelieu wing,
in rooms 18, 21 and 24.

1. Peter Paul Rubens, *The Arrival of Marie de' Medici at the Port of Marseille, 3 November 1600*, 1622-1625, oil on canvas, 394 x 295 cm
2. Peter Paul Rubens, *Hélène Fourment with a Carriage*, circa 1639, oil on wood, 195 x 132 cm
3. Anthony van Dyck, *Charles I, King of England, Out Hunting*, circa 1635-1638, oil on canvas, 266 x 207 cm

## *Rubens and van Dyck, european painters*

At the end of his life, Rubens painted his second wife and their children on a number of occasions, a sign of the domestic bliss and tenderness that he was then experiencing: he was a widow, aged fifty-three, when he married Hélène, then aged seventeen, who gave him several children.

After having worked in Rubens' studio, van Dyck travelled to Italy and England where he finally settled. In keeping with the tradition of Titian, this portrait of King Charles I, to whom he had been appointed official painter, helped van Dyck (who became known as "the Mozart of painting") to define aristocratic portraiture in England where he later had considerable influence.

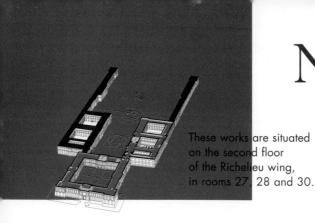

These works are situated
on the second floor
of the Richelieu wing,
in rooms 27, 28 and 30.

# NORTHERN
## PAINTINGS

1. Ambrosius Bosschaert, *Flower Bouquet in a Stone Arcature*,
   oil on copper, 23.5 x 17.5 cm
2. Frans Hals, *Jester with Lute*, circa 1624, oil on canvas, 70 x 62 cm
3. Frans Hals, *The Gypsy*, 1630, oil on wood, 58 x 52 cm

## *Portraits of figures and flowers*

**1**

Although the reasons for the immense popularity of floral paintings in the Netherlands from the end of the 16th century are not fully understood, this fondness for flowers was extremely well rooted. Florists' catalogues and sales contracts reveal totally extravagant prices - a tulip bulb could cost a good worker the equivalent of a year's wages - and in 1637, there was a major crash in the tulip trade which resulted in massive bankruptcy and gave rise to considerable moral reflection on the "vanity" of earthly possessions. Like other flower painters, Ambrosius Bosschaert evokes the transience of life by depicting a few withered leaves and insects, even though his flowers appear in all their splendour. Contrary to what one might think, these bouquets are unrealistic: the flowers in the bouquets used to come into bloom in different seasons. The painter thus never had this actual bouquet in front of him. Bosschaert's compositions are recognisable since they are often situated in a recess, with a background of blue sky.

**2**

By giving a lute to this figure painted with rapid, masterful brushstrokes, this image of a jester lies halfway between a genre scene and a realist portrait.

3 Frans Hals, who spent his whole life in Haarlem, painted nothing but portraits. In *The Gypsy*, his extremely free, wide brushstrokes, brilliantly rendering the fabric of the white blouse, truly craft his figure. This construction would have a lasting influence: it would be seen again in Fragonard's work, in his *"figures de fantaisie"* or fanciful figures, and in the 19th century, in Manet's work.

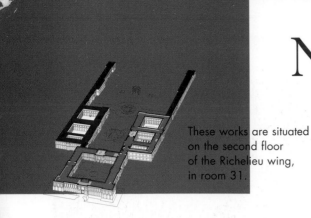

# NORTHERN PAINTINGS

1. Rembrandt Harmensz. van Rijn, known as Rembrandt, *Portrait of the Artist at His Easel*, 1660, oil on canvas, 111 x 90 cm
2. Rembrandt Harmensz. van Rijn, known as Rembrandt, *Philosopher Deep in Thought*, 1632, oil on wood, 28 x 34 cm
3. Rembrandt Harmensz. van Rijn, known as Rembrandt, *Bathsheba Bathing*, 1654, oil on canvas, 142 x 142 cm

## *Rembrandt, "the light" in painting*

**1** Rembrandt painted his hundred or so self-portraits throughout his career. This one shows him in the privacy of his studio: posing in his work clothes, holding his palette, brushes and maulstick, standing before a canvas placed on the easel. The light, which comes from the left, falls on the main parts of the painting: the painter's face and tools. At the end of his career, his palette became more sombre and was reduced to yellows, reds and browns. The thick, dense matter models the forms and, above all, the expression: painting makes it possible to express the inner movements of the mind more than it can say. It was the spiritual reality of the figures that would henceforth count.

**2** Next to a window with golden light flooding through, an old man sits with his hands clasped, meditating: perhaps the spiral staircase next to him evokes the twists and turns of his thoughts…

3 According to the Bible, King David, who had first perceived Bathsheba's beauty as she bathed, sent his messengers to summon her to his presence: Rembrandt thus took liberties with the text since he depicts Bathsheba with a letter from the king in her hand. Sitting on the right on a bench covered with fabric and a chemise, her head is slightly tilted forward, meditative and dreamy, seemingly ignoring the servant drying her feet. Her head and crossed legs are painted in profile whereas her torso is at an angle to the onlooker. Rembrandt scorned the canons of ideal beauty: Bathsheba's stomach is a little round, and her left arm rather long.

These works are situated
on the second floor
of the Richelieu wing,
in rooms 37 and 38.

# NORTHERN
## PAINTINGS

1. Pieter de Hooch, *Woman Drinking*, 1658, oil on canvas, 69 x 60 cm
2. Gerard Ter Borch, *The Duet: Singer and Theorbist*, 1669,
   oil on canvas, 82.5 x 72 cm
3. Johannes Vermeer, *The Lacemaker*, circa 1670-1671,
   oil on canvas glued onto wood, 23.9 x 20.5 cm
4. Johannes Vermeer, *The Astronomer*, 1668, oil on canvas, 51 x 45 cm

## *Vermeer and the "fine artists"*

**2**

Ter Borch helped to revive genre painting:
the mundane detail in his work, until then
fairly typical, in fact left room for a certain
refinement in scenes depicting domestic
and everyday intimacy. He thus joins the
ranks of the "fine artists" using precise,
distinct brushstrokes.

**1**

Most of De Hooch's paintings portray a series of rooms
through an open door: tiled or wooden floors, and beams on
the ceiling define the space in perspective. These genre
scenes in which a few figures drink, smoke or play music also
have a moral connotation: such pastimes may lead to romantic adventures…

**3**

"What Vermeer henceforth produced was no longer palpable substance, but the impalpable world of vision, a fundamentally separate world, evading reason," wrote Lawrence Gowing.

**4**

*The Astronomer* is one of Vermeer's few signed and dated canvases to have been preserved: the date in roman numerals and the artist's monogram are in fact on the door of the cabinet. Sat at his table covered with heavy cloth, the astronomer holds out his hand towards a celestial globe. The book in front of him has been identified: a treatise by Adriaen Metius, *On the Observation of Stars*, opened at the beginning of volume III. The composition of the canvas is very similar to that of another painting by Vermeer, also portraying a scholar at his work, *The Geographer:* with light entering through the window on the left, the scholar, absorbed in his thoughts, dominates a table behind which stands a cabinet. It is possible that the model in the two paintings was van Leeuwenhoek, the famous microscope-builder from Delft, who would later be appointed trustee of the Vermeer estate. In these two pieces, Vermeer moved away from his preferred theme: woman surprised in her domestic environment.

# NORTHERN PAINTINGS

These works are situated
on the second floor
of the Richelieu wing,
in room 8.

1. Hans Holbein, the Younger, *Erasmus*, 1523, oil on wood, 42 x 32 cm
2. Lucas Cranach, the Elder, *Venus*, 1529, oil on wood, 33 x 26 cm
3. Albrecht Dürer, *Self-portrait*, 1493, oil on parchment pasted onto canvas, 56.5 x 44.5 cm

## *Germanic painters*

**1** "I would like Dürer to paint my portrait; and why should I not ask this of such an artist?" wrote Erasmus. Is it unfortunate that this portrait of Erasmus was painted by Holbein, also a great portraitist of his contemporaries? Erasmus is portrayed in profile, similar to the images on antique medals, against a background composed of panelling and a wall-hanging with an oriental design. He wears a huge dark cloak and a black beret - it is known from his many letters that he was very sensitive to the cold. His face and hands, bathed in light, attract the gaze of the onlooker. His eyes are fixed on his page, Erasmus is absorbed in his writing: he would go down to posterity through his work. Holbein's painting thus became the classic image of the humanist at work.

**2** Whether part of mythology or biblical history, the women painted by Cranach in graceful landscapes are extremely refined: jewellery and hats give their nakedness a certain seductive charm.

3 During the 16th century, the Germanic countries boasted several leading painters, including Dürer, born in Nuremberg, a thriving cultural city, but still considerably marked by Gothic art. Through his numerous travels in Germany, the Netherlands and Italy, in particular, Dürer came into contact with the Renaissance which later influenced his painting. Throughout his career, he painted self-portraits in which he would pose, as seen here. The thistle stalk, a symbol of marital fidelity, which he holds in his right hand evokes, some say, his future marriage to Agnès Frey to whom the painting is said to have been given, while others say it is a symbol of Christ's passion, which is thought to confirm the inscription at the top of the painting meaning: "My life here on earth is how it has been ordained on high".

These works are situated
on the first floor
of the Denon wing,
in rooms 3 and 4.

1. Cenni di Pepi, known as Cimabue, *The Enthroned Virgin and Child Surrounded by Six Angels*, circa 1270, tempera on wood, 427 x 280 cm
2. Simone Martini, *The Bearing of the Cross*, circa 1335, tempera on wood, 28 x 16 cm
3. Giotto di Bondone, *Saint Francis of Assisi Receiving the Stigmata*, circa 1295-1300, tempera on wood, 313 x 163 cm

## *The great forerunners in Italy*

**1** The composition and attitude of the Virgin and Child enthroned in majesty (*Maestà* in Italian) correspond to Byzantine art: the figures, distributed symmetrically around a central axis on a gold background, are portrayed from the front, and their faces are devoid of expression. Nevertheless, a few tentative new details appear: the throne seen from the side and the folds of the mantle create both volume and depth, while the drapes covering the angels are fluid and loose. At the end of the 13th century, Cimabue thus started a real revolution in painting, which would be continued by Giotto. It is also said that Cimabue "discovered" Giotto painting sheep on a rock.

**2** This fragment of a small polyptych illustrates the art of this Sienese painter summoned to Avignon to the court of the Papacy. In a space saturated with figures, where the scale of the images portrayed is not preserved, the attitudes are highly characterised: Mary Magdalene with her raised open arms blatantly tells of her disarray.

**3** By choosing to paint precise moments from the life of Saint Francis of Assisi (1182-1226), his near-contemporary, Giotto introduced human finite space and time in his paintings, in relation to the eternity of God evoked by the gold backgrounds and the Byzantine figures conventionalised according to religious tradition. Using a more naturalistic style of painting, with sensitive emotion, expression, volume and perspective - indeed still rather clumsy, Giotto paves the way for Renaissance painting. A few traces of "archaism" still remain in this panel: the face of Christ is impassive and the landscape has not yet completely replaced the gold background.

# ITALIAN *PAINTINGS*

These works are situated
on the first floor
of the Denon wing,
in rooms 4 and 5.

1. Domenico Ghirlandaio, *Portrait of an Old Man and Young Boy*, circa 1488,
   tempera on wood, 63 x 46 cm
2. Antonio Pisano, known as Pisanello, *Portrait of Princess d'Este*, circa 1436-1438,
   oil on wood, 43 x 30 cm
3. Piero della Francesca, *Portrait of Sigismond Malatesta*, circa 1451,
   tempera and oil on wood, 44.5 x 34.5 cm

## *The primacy of the individual*

In the 15<sup>th</sup> century, princes and *condottieri*, both patrons and humanists, commissioned portraits from artists who travelled from court to court: namely the Este family in Ferrara, the Gonzague family in Mantua, the Montefeltre family in Urbino, and the Malatesta in Rimini… The painters still remained in the tradition of the profile, as depicted on ancient medals, a way of leaving the portrait to posterity.

**1** This realist portrait of the old man demonstrates the influence of Flemish painting in Florence at the end of the 15<sup>th</sup> century.

**2** Of course Pisanello, the great drawer, belonged to the Renaissance through his leaning towards Antiquity, which may be seen in his medal drafts. However, his connection with the international Gothic style is seen in the both precise and fluid lines which leave little room for the rendering of volume - as demonstrated here by the princess' shoulders or even her face which seem flat.

3 In this bust portrait, Piero della Francesca falls heir to the art of van der Weyden, as shown in the naturalistic rendering of the material and the play of light: Sigismond's slightly flushed cheek, the light catching on a few golden brocade threads and modelling his face. At the same time, the forms are geometrical: for example, his neck is reduced to a column. From this perspective, this painter, who was also a theoretician having written several treatises on perspective and proportions, joined the ranks of the great Renaissance thinkers, such as Alberti, for whom perfection initially stemmed from mathematical calculation. The work of Piero, who died in 1492, the year America was discovered, thus opened up a whole new realm in painting.

# ITALIAN
## *PAINTINGS*

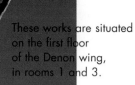

These works are situated
on the first floor
of the Denon wing,
in rooms 1 and 3.

1. Sandro di Mariano Filipepi, known as Botticelli, *Venus and the Graces Offering Gifts to a Young Girl*, circa 1480-1483, fresco, 211 x 283 cm
2. Guido di Pietro, known as Fra Angelico, *The Crowning of the Virgin*, circa 1430-1435, tempera on wood, 209 x 206 cm
3. Paolo di Dono, known as Uccello, *The Battle of San Romano*, circa 1455-1456, tempera on wood, 182 x 317 cm

## *The conquest of perspective*

1

Botticelli spent his whole working life in Florence, except for the period in Rome while working on the décor of the Sistine Chapel, and was very close to the Medici circle. This fresco decorated the loggia of a villa near Florence.

2

This altarpiece was painted for the Dominican monastery in Fiesole by Fra Angelico, a Dominican friar who painted the San Marco monastery in Florence. The magnificent colours and theme are still typical of medieval art. However, the composition based on a triangle and the circle made up of the assembly of saints, together with the mastery of space, determined by the interplay of the lines of the tiles and steps, belong to the Renaissance, established by Brunelleschi in terms of architecture, Masaccio in terms of painting, and Donatello as regards sculpture. Below the main scene, episodes from the life of Saint Dominic are depicted in the predella on either side of a suffering Christ.

3 This panel was part of a triptych which decorated the bedchamber of Laurent de' Medici at his palace in Florence. The scene describes one of the episodes of the battle in 1432: the counter-attack of the Florentines against the Sienese. The image is a mixture of archaism and modernity: while the knights and their horses, slightly stiff and rigid, are the archetype of disappearing medieval society, and the luxuriant detail and anecdotes belong to the Gothic tradition, the geometry of the horses' legs and the lances connects the artist, known as "the master of perspective", to his time.

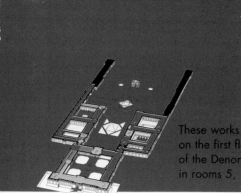

# ITALIAN
## *PAINTINGS*

These works are situated
on the first floor
of the Denon wing,
in rooms 5, 13 and 7.

1. Leonardo da Vinci, *The Virgin, the Child Jesus and Saint Anne*, circa 1508-1510, oil on wood, 168 x 130 cm
2. Leonardo da Vinci, *La Belle Ferronnière*, circa 1490-1495, oil on wood, 63 x 45 cm
3. Leonardo da Vinci, *Mona Lisa*, circa 1503-1506, oil on wood, 77 x 53 cm

## *Leonardo da Vinci*

After the first Florentine Renaissance, a period of "genius" began in Rome with Michelangelo, Raphael and Leonardo da Vinci, in turn architects, sculptors, painters, theoreticians and, sometimes, inventors.

**1** This theme, handled several times by Leonardo, is based on a dynamic pyramidal composition: the Virgin, on Saint Anne's knee, tries to hold on to the Child who is leaning towards the lamb, a sign foretelling his Passion. *Sfumato* and perspective give the scene a mysterious and supernatural feel, as is often the case in Leonardo's work.

**2** Whether this portrait bathed in light emerging from a dark background should be attributed to Leonardo is still debatable, as is the identity of the model.

3

This portrait is modelled by shade and light which comes both from the landscape and from the left. The artist's touch is fine and subtle: there is not a single trace of a brushmark. The lofty horizon opens onto a landscape where water, earth and air merge together, the different planes following on from each another through the aerial perspective - as the landscape moves further away, the colours change, from the range of reds to a more bluish palette. The contours of the Mona Lisa leaning on a balustrade have been softened: Leonardo's famous *sfumato*. "Contours are the least important feature… Therefore, dear painter, do not define your figures with a line," affirms Leonardo who aims not to describe the features of the Mona Lisa precisely, but rather to paint her soul, with sensitivity in her gaze and her enigmatic smile. Hung in Bonaparte's bedchamber, the *Mona Lisa* was then exhibited at the Louvre where it attracted much notice. Stolen in 1911, and vandalised in 1956, the painting would be the subject of numerous variations by 20th century artists thus revealing their fascination for the piece, in their own unique way.

1 A man of letters and ambassador to the court of Urbino, the town where Raphael was born, Baldassare Castiglione was the painter's friend and counsellor, as shown in their correspondence. This portrait illustrates the essence of the perfect gentleman, as defined by Castiglione in his work, *The Courtier*, which became a best-seller throughout Europe in his time. The "distinguished" man is solemn, kind, and identifiable by his bearing alone. The limited palette emphasises his lightly coloured face and, above all, his blue eyes which make him very present - apparently, he seemed so alive that children often wanted to embrace him. The blended brush-stroke on the fine canvas, covered with a very thin preparation, probably helps to create the vibrancy of the figure, lit by diffused light. Raphael painted this portrait in Rome: summoned in 1508 by Pope Julius II to decorate his apartments at the Vatican, he was appointed architect of Saint Peter's in 1514, and then became the controller of antiquities. He died there prematurely, at the age of thirty-seven.

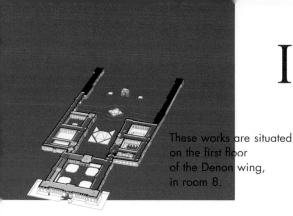

These works are situated on the first floor of the Denon wing, in room 8.

# ITALIAN
## *PAINTINGS*

1. Raffaello Sanzio, known as Raphael, *Baldassare Castiglione*, 1514-1515, oil on canvas, 82 x 67 cm
2. Raffaello Sanzio, known as Raphael, *Half-length portrait of a woman*, circa 1504-1505, pen and brown ink, 22.3 x 15.9 cm
3. Raffaello Sanzio, known as Raphael, *The Virgin and Child with Saint John the Baptist*, also known as *La Belle Jardinière*, 1507, oil on wood, 122 x 80 cm

## *Raphael*

2 Raphael was also a great drawer. Like in the portrait of *Baldassare Castiglione*, the figure here poses in the same way as the *Mona Lisa* - evidently, Leonardo greatly influenced the young Raphael.

3 The Virgin's elaborate hairstyle and gentle expression correspond to the Florentine tradition. However, this does not lessen the intensity of the scene set in a peaceful landscape, probably due to the attitude and the glances exchanged between the three protagonists arranged according to a classical pyramidal structure: attentive and contemplative, the Virgin and Saint John the Baptist both have their eyes fixed on the Child. The latter attempts to take hold of the book, announcing his Passion, placed on the virgin's arm, while Saint John the Baptist holds the cross, another sign foreshadowing the future sacrifice.

77

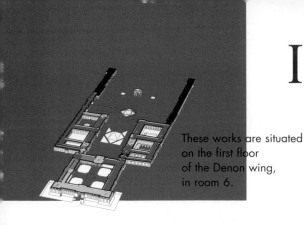

# ITALIAN
## *PAINTINGS*

These works are situated
on the first floor
of the Denon wing,
in room 6.

1. Tiziano Vecellio, known as Titian (attributed to), *Pastoral Concert*, circa 1510-1511, oil on canvas, 105 x 136.5 cm
2. Tiziano Vecellio, known as Titian, *Man with Glove*, circa 1520-1523, oil on canvas, 100 x 89 cm
3. Paolo Caliari, known as Veronese, *The Wedding at Cana*, 1562-1563, oil on canvas, 666 x 990 cm

## *16th-century Venice*

**1** The subject of the painting and the artist's technique have both helped to support the doubts concerning the attribution of the painting, either to Giorgione in his last years (he died of the plague in 1510), or to the young Titian. Although the meaning of the painting remains a mystery, certain themes used in Venetian painting at the time are still present - romantic banter in a pastoral setting and music.

**2** A hundred or so portraits by Titian have been preserved, some anonymous like this one, but also portraits of the most well-known figures of the time, the Gonzague family, François I, Charles Quint, and Philippe II of Spain. Titian was not content to merely depict the physical and psychological characteristics of his models, but was also able to represent how they imagined themselves and their role. His brush therefore paints a little of their soul...

**3** This enormous canvas was commissioned in 1562, for the refectory of the Benedictine monastery of San Giorgio Maggiore which had been rebuilt by Palladio. The pictorial space is perfectly incorporated into the actual space: the ground and columns in the painting extend the architecture of the room, an arrange-ment in keeping with Vitruvius' writings. The pictorial area is too vast to be taken in at a glance, and numerous vanishing points coexist: one corresponding to the figures and thc other, in the upper part, draw-ing the onlooker's eye towards the sky which opens the refectory space to the outside. Veronese thus appears as a great decorator, filling his canvas with figures in contemporary costumes and objects bearing no direct relation to the scene described in the Gospel, which church censors would criticise him for in another canvas. Veronese would retort "Let us, painters, take the same liberties as poets and madmen," freely quoting from the poet Horace.

These works are situated
on the first floor
of the Denon wing,
in room 12.

# ITALIAN
## *PAINTINGS*

1. Michelangelo Merisi, known as Caravaggio,
*The Fortune-teller*, circa 1594, oil on canvas,
99 x 131 cm
2. Michelangelo Merisi, known as Caravaggio,
*The Death of the Virgin*, 1605-1606,
oil on canvas, 369 x 245 cm

## *A great innovator: Caravaggio*

**1**

The fortune-teller is about to rob this elegant, but naive,
young man: she is trying to spirit away his ring with her
right hand. This painting is typical of Caravaggio's first
paintings evoking genre scenes: elegant young men
playing music or in front of a basket of fruit. This aspect
of Caravaggio's work would be much copied, in France,
northern Holland and, of course, in Italy, at the beginning
of the 17th century.

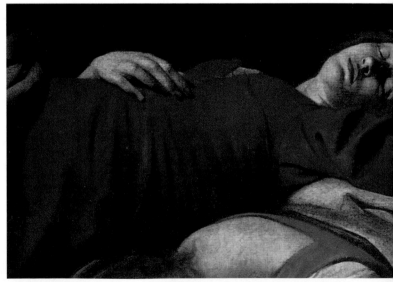

**2**

When Caravaggio delivered his large painting to the discalced
Carmelites who had commissioned the piece for their church in
Rome, it was rejected due to indecency. However, Rubens, then in
Italy at the court of Mantua, advised the duke, his patron, to purchase the painting for his collection. The friars criticised Caravaggio
for having made the Virgin look like a real corpse - the painter is
thought to have used a drowned prostitute for his model, hence the
Virgin's body is very white and bloated. Depicting the Virgin in this
way challenges the idea that she was taken to heaven the moment
she died. The painter emphasises the drama and the pain of the dis-
ciples with the stream of light cutting diagonally across the painting. Shortly after having completed this piece, Caravaggio, accu-
sed of murder, was forced to flee Rome.

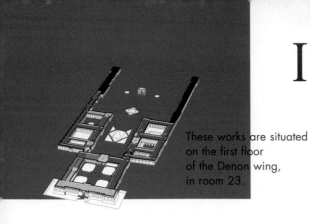

These works are situated
on the first floor
of the Denon wing,
in room 23.

# ITALIAN
## *PAINTINGS*

1. Giandomenico Tiepolo, *Christ and the Adulteress*,
   1751, oil on canvas, 84 x 105 cm
2. Giandomenico Tiepolo, *Carnival Scene*, circa 1754-1755,
   oil on canvas, 80 x 110 cm
3. Francesco Guardi, *The Departure of the Bucentaure for the Venice Lido,
   on Ascension Day*, 1766-1770, oil on canvas, 66 x 101 cm

## *18<sup>th</sup>-century Venice*

**1** Giandomenico was the last of the 18<sup>th</sup>-century Venetian painters to travel throughout Europe: he and his father to Würzburg and Madrid, Canaletto to London, and Bellotto to central Europe. He died in 1804, after having seen the end of an era: seven years previously the Treaty of Campo Formio placed the Venetian Republic under Austrian protection.

**2** How could the son and nephew of two great artists, Giambattista Tiepolo and Francesco Guardi, avoid becoming a painter? Although Giandomenico began his career in his father's studio and accompanied him on some of his important decorating assignments far from his native Venice, he subsequently moved towards painting everyday life demonstrating great narrative inventiveness and tinged with a touch of irony.

3   This canvas is part of a series of twelve paintings (ten in the Louvre) illustrating the festivities organised in Venice in honour of the election of the Doge Alviso IV Mocenigo. Painted approximately ten years after the ceremonies, they were inspired by etched compositions after Antonio Canaletto. This painting corresponds to the departure of the Bucentaure galley for the Lido where the doge celebrated the union of Venice and the Adriatic on Ascension Day each year. This scene was an excuse for Guardi to paint a view of Venice and its inhabitants in translucent silvery light, with his quivering, airy brushstroke, and completely new sensitivity to the atmosphere. Guardi thus completely revived *veduta*, the painting or drawing of a place, by replacing the precise view of his predecessor and compatriot, Canaletto, with a more poetic or even fantastic vision.

Next page:
Francesco Guardi,
*The Doge of Venice at the Festivities on the*
*Thursday before Shrove Tuesday on the Piazetta*,
1766-1770, oil on canvas, 67 x 100 cm

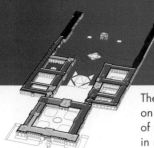

These works are situated
on the first floor
of the Denon wing,
in rooms 29 and 30.

1. Domenikos Theotocopoulos, known as El Greco, *Christ on the Cross Adored by Two Donors*, circa 1585-1590, oil on canvas, 260 x 171 cm
2. Bartolomé Esteban Murillo, *The Beggar Boy*, circa 1650, oil on canvas, 134 x 100 cm
3. Francisco de Zurbarán, *Saint Apollinia*, circa 1635-1640, oil on canvas, 116 x 66 cm
4. Francisco José de Goya y Lucientes, *Portrait of the Countess del Carpio, Marquise of La Solana*, 1794-1795, oil on canvas, 181 x 122 cm

## *Painting on the other side of the Pyrenees*

The Spanish collections at the Louvre, now fairly modest, once boasted more than four hundred paintings when Louis-Philippe created his famous "Spanish Museum". The collection was dispersed after the July Monarchy.

**2**

In this piece on youth, Murillo handles one of his frequent recurring themes, Andalusian urchins hanging about the streets, with little to eat - some melons or a few prawns here and there, a picaresque theme which also exists in literature. The same artist would later paint multiple images of the Immaculate Conception, the sweetness of which is the opposite extreme of the brutal realist chiaroscuro of this scene.

**3**

Zurbarán painted numerous elegant full-length portraits of saints, often recognisable through their gestures or the attributes they hold, alluding to their martyrdom. Here, Apollinia holds a tooth in a pair of pincers.

**1**

"I had already seen some of his paintings which I found extremely striking… If my figures tended to be elongated during my blue period, it is probably due to his influence" (Picasso in a letter to Brassaï).

4

"The world is a farce; faces, clothes and voices; the whole thing is an illusion. Every man wants to seem something he is not, everyone deceives, and no one knows himself". Thus spoke Goya, who was able, however, to communicate the strength of character of this charitable, cultivated woman, who was still young but very unwell and, knowing herself to be terminally ill, undoubtedly wished to leave her daughter this portrait. Having barely recovered from a long illness which left him deaf, Goya henceforth adopted a lively spontaneous touch, similar to that used in a sketch, which would be criticised by the supporters of "academic" painting.

These works are situated
on the second floor
of the Richelieu wing.

1. Joseph Mallord William Turner, *Landscape with River and Distant Bay*, circa 1845, oil on canvas, 93.5 x 123.5 cm
2. John Constable, *View of Salisbury*, circa 1820, oil on canvas, 35.5 x 51.5 cm
3. Thomas Gainsborough, *Conversation in a Park*, circa 1746-1747, oil on canvas, 73 x 68 cm
4. Joshua Reynolds, *Master Hare*, circa 1788-1789, oil on canvas, 77 x 63 cm

## *Painting across the Channel*

**1** On 18 February 1890, Edmond de Goncourt wrote on the subject of this painting, which Turner himself did not consider a finished work but rather a study: "An afternoon spent in front of Groult's British paintings… One of the canvases was a Turner: an ethereal bluish lake, with undefined contours, a distant lake, in a flash of electric light, right at the end of golden-brown terrain. In God's name! It makes you despise Monet's inventiveness and the other innovators of his kind!"

**2** British artists' mastery of watercolour in the 19th century enabled them to paint extremely expressive landscapes from life. Moreover, Constable was in the habit of painting outside using oils which, at the time, was very uncommon - he often wrote notes on his sketches, indicating the wind direction, and the weather… His work is punctuated by numerous series based on the same theme: he thus aimed to reproduce the atmosphere, the sky and light through the seasons.

3

"We will all go to Paradise and van Dyck will be one of the party." These words spoken by the dying Gainsborough to his contemporary and rival, Reynolds, who had come to visit him, clearly reveal the influence of the Flemish painter across the Channel. *Conversation in a Park* illustrates the two genres which Gainsborough painted throughout his life: the landscape and the portrait, brought together here to depict, perhaps, the painter and his wife.

4

This portrait, painted with such free brushstrokes that it has sometimes been considered a sketch, is of a two-year-old boy. Reynolds, who was the most sought-after portraitist in London - commanding higher prices than Gainsborough, often painted images of children.

# GRAPHIC ARTS

1. Antonio Pisano, known as Pisanello, *Two Harnessed Horses, seen at an angle, one from the front and the other from the back*, pre-1438-1439, pen and brown ink, grey and brown wash tints, white highlights, preparatory lines drawn in *pierre noire* or lead pencil, 19.9 x 16.5 cm
2. Peter Paul Rubens, *Landscape with Fallen Tree,* 17th century, *pierre noire*, drawn over in pen and brown ink, 58.2 x 48.9 cm
3. Jacques-Louis David, *Queen Marie-Antoinette Going to the Scaffold*, 1793, pen and brown ink, 14.8 x 10.1 cm
4. Eugène Delacroix, *Morocco Diary*, 1832, hardback album, covered with dark-green paper, comprising fifty-six rough sketches in graphite, pen and brown ink, often accompanied with watercolour highlights and handwritten notes, 16.5 x 9.8 cm

*Pen and ink, graphite, pierre noire, wash tints...*

**1**  Horses, goldfinches, camels, eagles, grasshoppers, guinea-fowl, swans, monkeys, jays, turtledoves, kingfishers, deer, herons, budgerigars, chamois, foxes, stags, rabbits, cheetahs, bears, dromedaries, goats, tortoises, rams, greyhounds, pigeons, partridges, teals, hoopoes... There is no end to the list of animals included in the work of Pisanello, who drew them from every angle and in every position. Here, the skilled use of foreshortening and the fineness of the model defined by subtle shading demonstrate the immense art of Pisanello the drawer, renowned for his skill as a medal engraver.

**2**  Rubens, who showed little interest in landscape painting, sketched the two trees with spirit and tension: the uprooted fallen tree in the foreground gives the landscape a tragic dimension.

**3** With a few strokes of a pen, David sketched the queen, resigned and dignified, shortly before her execution. According to an inscription accompanying the drawing, David is said to have seen the procession from a window.

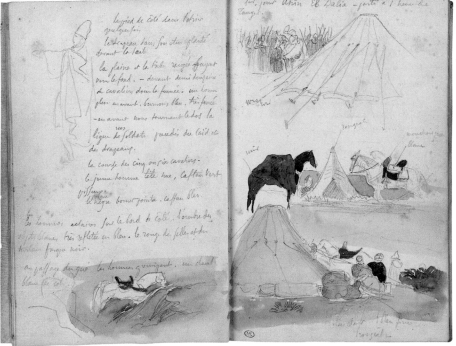

**4** "We were Hellenists in the age of Louis XIV, but now we are Orientalists," wrote Victor Hugo in *Les Orientales*. Delacroix did not escape this fashion. He travelled through North Africa from January to June 1832: he managed to join the Duke de Mornay's mission, sent by Louis-Philippe to the Sultan of Morocco. He thus noted and drew everything he saw in his diaries, in a disorderly fashion, clearly demonstrating his excitement in the discovery of such strange places.

# SCULPTURES

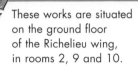

These works are situated
on the ground floor
of the Richelieu wing,
in rooms 2, 9 and 10.

1. *The Dead Christ*, first half of the 12<sup>th</sup> century, wood, h: 155 cm
2. *Tomb of Philippe Pot*, originating from the church of Cîteaux (the Gold Coast),
   end of the 15<sup>th</sup> century, painted stone, h: 182 cm
3. Jean de Liège, *Tomb containing the entrails of King Charles IV Le Bel
   and Jeanne d'Evreux*, 1372, marble, h: 110 cm

*The omnipresence of death in the Middle Ages*

**1** The position of Christ's right arm rules out a Crucifixion: this Christ is probably the only preserved part of a Descent from the Cross. Traces of polychromy show that these pieces, which today seem rather bare, were originally painted.

**2** This tomb was carved for Philippe Pot, the great seneschal of Burgundy. It is in the form of a funeral procession. The mourners which used to decorate the walls of the tombs now actually carry the stone slab supporting the recumbent statue.

3 During the 14$^{th}$ century, it became common practice for kings and queens to envisage dividing their body after their death: the future deceased could therefore choose several different burial sites according to pious, sentimental or political criteria. This is what Charles IV and Jeanne d'Evreux requested in their last will and testament. This tomb shows them smaller than life. The sceptre that they once held in their right hand has now disappeared, while on their chest is a small bag containing their entrails. The traditional animals at their feet symbolise strength and loyalty: a lion and a lioness, and two dogs.

# SCULPTURES

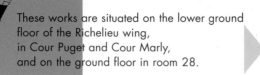

These works are situated on the lower ground floor of the Richelieu wing, in Cour Puget and Cour Marly, and on the ground floor in room 28.

1. Pierre Puget, *Milo of Crotona*, 1682, marble, h: 270 cm
2. Jean-Antoine Houdon, *Voltaire*, antique bust, bronze, h: 35.5 cm
3. Guillaume I Coustou, *The Escaped Horses Held Back by the Grooms*, known as *Horses of Marly*, 1743-1745, marble, h: 355 cm

## *French sculpture and naturalism*

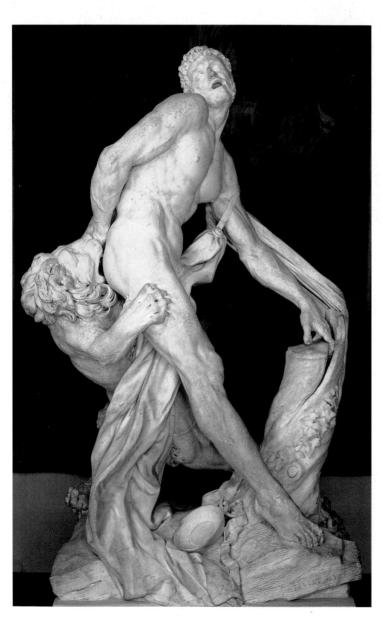

**1**

"The poor man, how he suffers!" exclaimed Queen Marie-Antoinette when the group carved by Puget (1620-1694), an artist trained very early on in Italy and who spent almost his whole life outside the Parisian circles, was erected in the estate of the Château de Versailles. He illustrates the destiny of Milo an athlete who won the ancient Olympian games, who, already old, wanted to measure his strength by splitting the trunk of an oak tree. However, he had lost his vitality: the tree closed on his hand, and he was finally devoured by wolves - in this case, a lion. In a century still greatly marked by French classicism consisting of grandeur, ideals and balance, Puget, the most baroque of all the 17th-century French sculptors, particularly emphasises the suffering of the hero: Milo braces his body, his mouth wide open screams with pain, and his toes claw at the ground.

**2**

Houdon (1741-1828) spent fifty or so years producing numerous portraits of his contemporaries, succeeding not only in conveying their facial features but also capturing their personality.

**3**

The *Horses of Marly*, carved by Guillaume I Coustou were intended to replace the equestrian groups devised by his uncle Antoine Coysevox to decorate the horse-pond at the Château de Marly, which had been taken to the gardens of the Palais Royal des Tuileries. Here, it is the naturalistic rendering of the horses which predominates the piece: rearing horses with streaming manes and quivering nostrils. Erected at the foot of the Champs-Elysées since the year II, they were returned to the Louvre in 1984, and replaced by casts.

# SCULPTURES

These works are situated
on the lower ground floor
of the Denon wing, in room C,
and on the ground floor in room 4.

1. Antonio Canova, *Psyche Revived by Cupid's Kiss*, 1793, marble, h: 155 cm
2. Gregor Erhart, *Mary Magdalene*, beginning of the 16th century,
   polychrome lime, h: 177 cm
3. Michelangelo Buonarroti, known as Michelangelo, *Slave*, known as *Dying Slave*,
   1513-1515, unfinished marble, h: 228 cm

## Sculpture in Italy and Germany

1 Canova went to Rome at the age of twenty-two: artists and art lovers went in search of not only ancient Rome but also the great masters of the Renaissance. It was there that Canova soon became the herald of ideal beauty, as redefined by the theoreticians of neo-classicism.

2 This *Mary Magdalene* was probably intended to be seen from all sides: her back is also carefully carved and painted. It is possible that she originally hung from the vault of a church and was surrounded by angels. According to the legend, while she withdrew naked to a grotto in order to repent, angels transported her to heaven every day to hear a concert of celestial music. Even though painted locks of hair were originally added to the carved hair, to hide her nakedness, a certain sensuality, which heralds the Renaissance, emanates from this figure.

3    From Bramante and Michelangelo to Raphael, Julius II managed to attract the greatest artists in his time to work on grandiose projects for the greater glory of the Pope and the Church. In 1505, he commissioned Michelangelo to devise a project for his tomb destined for Saint Peter's Basilica, the rebuilding of which had, moreover, commenced. However, the project was interrupted since Michelangelo was charged with decorating the ceiling of the Sistine Chapel. When he returned to his task, the initial project had been greatly simplified. The two *Slaves* in the Louvre were intended for the base of the tomb. In *Dying Slave*, the skilled anatomical rendering - the work on the fingers of the right hand is remarkable - perhaps leaves more room for an impression of quietness and mystery.

# OBJETS D'ART

These works are situated on the first floor
of the Richelieu wing and the Sully section.

1. *Barberini Ivory*, Constantinople, first half of the 6<sup>th</sup> century, ivory, h: 34 cm
2. *Descent from the Cross*, Paris studio, second half of the 13<sup>th</sup> century, ivory, h: 29 cm
3. *Suger's Eagle*, Egypt or Imperial Rome (vase) and pre-1147 (setting), porphyry and gilded silver, h: 43 cm
4. *Virgin of Jeanne d'Evreux*, pre-1339, gilded silver and enamel, h: 68 cm

## Pious objects from the Middle Ages

**1** The triumphant emperor on horseback, in the centre and in bold relief, dominates the submissive peoples offering him tributes, beneath the watchful eye of the bust of Christ bestowing a blessing. The master of the heavenly realm witnesses the triumph of the emperor who reigns on earth.

**2** The figures in this *Descent from the Cross* show deep emotion, but without excessive pathos – although Christ's head is upside down, his hair remains on his shoulders. This piece demonstrates the level of quality achieved by Parisian ivory carvers in the 13<sup>th</sup> century.

**3**

When Abbot Suger discovered an ancient porphyry vase in a chest, he had the idea of transforming it into a liturgical vessel in the shape of an eagle. According to him, nothing was too beautiful to glorify God, and even luxury and beauty were a way of reaching God.

**4**

Queen Jeanne d'Evreux, wife of Charles IV, gave this Virgin to the Abbey of Saint-Denis. The sinuous outline of the Virgin, extended widthwise with its large draping folds on the side, is characteristic of the Gothic period. The silversmith's immense technical virtuosity did not prevent him showing great sensitivity: the Virgin's face is a little sad and pensive while the child's gesture is marked with tenderness. The figures are placed on a pedestal composed of fourteen enamelled plaques illustrating scenes from Christ's childhood and his Passion.

These works are situated on the first floor
of the Richelieu wing and the Sully section.

1. Jean-Baptiste Boulard, *Queen's Wing Chair*, 1789, white-painted beech, h: 96 cm
2. *Crown used in the coronation of Louis XV*, 1722, treasure from the Abbey of Saint-Denis, gilded silver, reproduction precious stones and embroidered satin
3. André Charles Boulle, *Cabinet*, circa 1700, oak frame, ebony and amaranth veneer, inlaid brass, pewter, horn, tortoiseshell and coloured wood, gilded bronze, h: 255.5 cm

## *French cabinetwork*

The famous 140-carat Regent diamond, acquired by Duke Philippe d'Orléans at the beginning of the 18th century, adorned this crown during the coronation of Louis XV.

**1**

This wing chair was part of the furniture from the Château de Montreuil, situated in Versailles, which King Louis XVI gave to his sister, Madame Elisabeth - who was responsible for the rose-motif crewelwork. It was commissioned, with a whole series of chairs, at the end of 1788, by Thierry de Ville d'Avray, general intendant of the Crown furniture, who was, however, hesitant to do so since France was in a poor economic situation.

**3**

Boulle, who became "cabinetmaker, engraver, gilder and sculptor to the king" in 1672, brought floral inlaid work and an inlay technique known as Boullework, already practised in Germany but which he would develop to its peak, into line with current tastes. This two-door cabinet combines both techniques. Inlaid wood was used for the two large vases of flowers on the doors; the compartments above and below correspond to Boullework. This technique consists in cutting a given motif in two superimposed sheets of different materials, one light and the other dark - brass, pewter, horn and tortoiseshell. The motif from one is then inserted into the other in order to obtain two sheets with an identical motif, the colour of which is reversed.

# AFRICA, ASIA, OCEANIA
# AND THE AMERICAS

These works are situated on the ground floor of the Denon wing, in rooms 1 to 5.

1. *Royal mask (tukah)*, Bamendou kingdom, Bamileke plateau, Cameroon grassland, first half of the 19<sup>th</sup> century, wood, h: 86 cm
2. *Statue of the god Rao*, Mangareva Island, Gambier archipelago, 10<sup>th</sup> century (?), wood, h: 106 cm
3. *Head from Ife*, 12<sup>th</sup>-14<sup>th</sup> century, Nigeria, terracotta, 15.5 cm

This mask was carved from a single piece of wood. It represents a founding ancestor of the chieftaincy. In this region, ancestors are represented with a domed forehead and bulging cheeks deliberately evoking a torso, thighs and a potent sex organ, a symbol of fertility. In the openwork tiara above the face, lizards are connected with the world of the dead. This extremely heavy mask, which was probably held at arm's length, was only brought out during special ceremonies.

At the beginning of the 19<sup>th</sup> century, missionaries set about converting this region of Oceania: during this rapid mass "conversion" - which took place over a period of two years, temples and ritualistic objects were destroyed. This statue is therefore a survivor: it was part of a collection of objects sent to France as an "educational" testimony to pagan beliefs. It is difficult to support a global theory on the rites and beliefs of these peoples. It is nevertheless thought that the statues did not personify divinities, but merely represented them. This is said to partly explain the ease with which missionaries were able to organise immense autos-da-fé: for the natives, these images were empty.

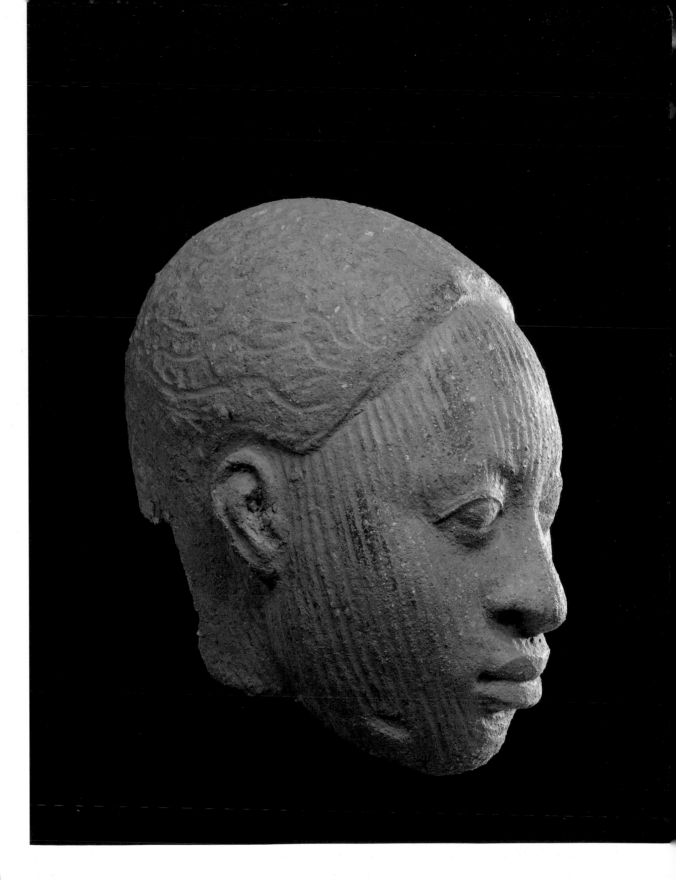

**3** This head originated from Ife, considered by the Yoruba as their spiritual and cultural capital. When the German ethnologist, Leo Frobenius, discovered them, he refused to believe that this head, and others, made of terracotta and bronze, could be the work of African artists - different theories were devised involving European artists washed up on African shores who supposedly founded a school! However, these heads were crafted before even the first contact with Europeans. They mostly represent the *oni*, meaning "king", but also members of his family or entourage. The dimensions of this head, smaller than life, are said to represent one of the king's servants: they recapture the subject's idealised features.

*Grand drawing-room in Napoleon III's suite,* 1856-1861

This grand drawing-room was part of a magnificent suite of reception rooms, incorrectly known as "the Duke de Morny's suite" since it was neither commissioned nor lived in by the duke. Imitation marbles, paintings, an abundance of gold, sculptural décor, damask hangings, gilt wooden chairs, chandeliers and candelabras all contributed to the stately, majestic effect of the decorative style of the Second Empire, very few reminders of which have been preserved.

Achevé d'imprimer
le 31 mai 2005
Dépôt légal juin 2005
Imprimé par Impression Presses de Bretagne Service